100 CREATIVE PRAYER IDEAS FOR CHILDREN

100 Creative Prayer Ideas for Children

JAN DYER

KINGSWAY PUBLICATIONS
EASTBOURNE

Unless otherwise indicated, biblical quotations are
from the Good News Bible © American Bible Society 1976,
published by Bible Society and HarperCollins.

Biblical quotations marked NIV are taken from
the New International Version © 1973, 1978, 1984
by the International Bible Society.

Biblical quotations marked NCV are taken from
the New Century Version (Anglicised Edition)
The Youth Bible copyright © 1993 Nelson Word.

Suggested songs are from *Songs of Fellowship for Kids* (SOFK)
and *Junior Praise* (JP)

ISBN 0 85476 778 9

Published by
KINGSWAY PUBLICATIONS
Lottbridge Drove, Eastbourne, E Sussex BN23 6NT.
E-mail: books@kingsway.co.uk

Designed and produced for the publishers by
Bookprint Creative Services, P.O. Box 827, BN21 3YJ, England.
Printed in Great Britain.

Contents

Acknowledgements

A special thank you to my husband Graham and to our children, Rachel, Hannah and Rebekah, for all the fun times we have had praying together. Writing this book has been a family project, so I would like to thank Rachel, Hannah and Rebekah for their help with suggestions, writing prayers, rhymes and raps, illustrations, typing and reading parts of the manuscript and, on occasions, getting their own tea!

I would also like to thank the children in Stopwatch Club and in the Sunday groups of Christ Church, Lye, and the children who have been in Pebbles at the Soul Survivor and New Wine Lakeside Conferences, who have shared in many of these prayer ideas before writing a book was even thought about. Thanks also to Tearfund for inspiring Idea 60; to Amanda Grey Smart for allowing me to use her idea based on snooker balls (Idea 70); to the Revd David Woodhouse for the prayer in Idea 2; to Emma Towers-Evan and her mum for giving me permission to share their experiences of prayer (see Idea 3); to Peter Sutherland and his dad for their contributions to Part One; and Hannah and Rachel's friends, Hannah George, Paul Eades, Tim Corbett and Chris Prosser for their help with the illustrations.

I have sought permission, where appropriate, for the inclusion of prayer ideas that are not my own. Idea 56 has come from an organisation involved in mission, but I cannot trace its origin. The reader may also be aware that some of my suggestions are adaptations of ideas that have been around for many years and their original source may not be known.

Finally, thank you to so many friends for their support and encouragement, especially Margaret who helped me to plan the format of the book and read much of the manuscript, and to Mary and Jo for their reading and constructive comments.

PART ONE

Children and Prayer

Introduction

Dad: Did you have a good night, son?
Peter: Yes thanks, Dad, but I cheated.
Dad: What do you mean . . . you cheated?
Peter: I asked God to help me.

(Peter Sutherland, age 7)

Prayer is a natural thing for our children to do. What is prayer? It is talking with our heavenly Father anytime, anywhere. What is talking? It's communicating. We can communicate with words (spoken or written) and in other ways too, like pictures, body language, movement, dance, drawing, craftwork, singing, music, silence and rest.

Our God is a God of creativity. He created the heavens and the earth. He moved across the face of the waters. He breathed new life into his creation. And so it is with our children. Children are creative beings, made in the image of a creator God, and they enjoy their creativity. They can say with God, 'It is good' (cf. Genesis 1).

This book is divided into three parts. Part One looks at praying in different settings, and is intended as an overview rather than an in-depth study. You may like to select the sections that most interest you.

Praying children

Children can pray ... for themselves, for their parents and family, for their friends, for their schools, for concerns in the nation and overseas. The age of the child and their experience of the situation will determine how able they are to pray. A few years ago, I was deeply moved by a four-year-old's prayer for the street children in Guatemala – children among whom she had lived for three years and who were her friends.

Prayer helps us to think about others. It develops a caring heart within our children, helping them to become aware of others and their needs. As they see the needs of others being met through their prayers, their faith is built up.

Children learn too that God is not a grand Father Christmas, and he does not give us all that we ask in the way we might want. God knows our needs and the needs of those for whom we pray. Yet he is a God who answers prayer, for he has ordained prayer. Prayer does change things. The impossible is made possible. Prayer is a partnership involving our working with God.

How can we help children pray?

We can teach children to say 'thank you', 'sorry' and 'please' to God in the same way that we teach them to say these things to us. We can help them to forgive others and themselves. This is not always easy, and it's all right for children to know that they can be honest with God and tell him that they are finding this hard. They can ask God to help them to want to forgive.

I remember hearing forgiveness likened to the healing of a wound. If you cut yourself, the wound needs to be cleaned and healing starts with the inner layers, working outwards to the surface of the skin. The depth of the wound determines how long the healing process will take. It also helps in the forgiving process if the person who has hurt us is able to say 'sorry'!

In helping children to pray, we need to see the world through the eyes of a child. Although we have all been children, this isn't as easy as it sounds. It may have been a long time ago, and even if it wasn't, the world of children keeps changing. In trying to see things their way, we need to come alongside children and use our imagination. Who knows? Maybe you'll become as imaginative as the children in your care?

The focus of this book is to help you to think creatively, to use the experiences of children through their play and interactions in such a way as to stimulate them into readily talking to God. As children grow up, their games change and their friendships deepen. Their relationship with God changes too. But the constant objective remains the same: to encourage children to enjoy being in the presence of God, with this relationship being a natural two-way conversation, a meaningful and lasting friendship that will become central to their lives and stay with them as they grow up.

Praying in the family

Family prayer times can be a source of stress or delight. In our household we have passed through different phases, but the main constant has been the habit of praying at mealtimes. This is accepted and expected, and the older children are now in their mid and late teens. The prayers have changed from singing to speaking, and breakfast is now more a do-it-yourself affair and more likely to be taken on the run, but the main meal of the day is eaten together and provides opportunity for family togetherness and information exchange.

Stresses arise when we are bored with or embarrassed by the way we are praying as a family. Being sensitive to this and talking about it can overcome this difficulty. Sometimes a change of approach is what is needed, or maybe even a break. Spending time with each of the children individually as well as altogether as a family, taking them out on a special treat, praying with the children by themselves, and keeping confidences, all support our bonding as a family and aid our prayer and worship together. If we can share something of our lives with the children, this enables them to pray for us as well. It is healthy for them to know that grown-ups have prayer needs and that they can pray for their parents.

Our greatest delight has been to invite those visiting us to join us for family prayers. Our visitors tell us that these times have been special for them too, and all of us have been blessed.

Praying with others

Older children and teenagers can also develop listening skills and support each other as they pray together. They can be given the same kind of guidelines for prayer ministry as adults in the church. Younger children too can be encouraged to pray for other children or with adults as part of the prayer ministry team. Parents of very young children have shared how the Lord has answered the prayers of their young children of three and four as they have prayed for their parents. Let us not be afraid to allow our children to pray with us and for us.

Church prayer meeting

In theory children can attend the church prayer meeting, but there are a number of factors which make this difficult, not least the time of the meeting and the expectations of adults. Prayer meetings often start at 8 pm, which is not a good time for children to be out; nor does sitting quietly in a circle suit their energy and active nature. But children can meet to pray. One of our children, at the age of twelve, felt the Lord speak to her about this. The outworking was a children's prayer group. Children in our church join together by choice to find out about and pray for other children, including those in other nations. Children can also meet as prayer buddies in twos or threes, and this encourages their praying.

Personal prayer times

Personal prayer times are a valuable habit for children to develop, and one which can be started early in life. Parents often sing their babies to sleep, and to use soothing Christian songs is one way of praying over them. As they grow older, stories are often read at bedtimes. These can be stories from the Bible. There are some really good Bibles available today, designed for young children. We found with our youngest daughter that she could 'read' her Bible before she could read. Encouraging this has a double advantage. It gives children confidence in pre-reading and it enables them to learn from the Scriptures.

As the child grows older, Bible reading notes can be added to the Bible time, and these will also give ideas for prayer. Encouraging the child to pray out loud develops confidence in praying. Children may prefer to pray in their heads or write their prayers down in their prayer books. It is important for us to respect their choice. We are there to encourage and help them to grow in their relationship with God. This involves allowing them to take more responsibility for their personal times with the Lord.

Maintaining our own personal times with the Lord is

important for our children. We all know how they watch us, and if they see how important it is for us to talk to our Father God, then doing this for themselves will take a higher priority. Now that our eldest daughter is seventeen, we use the same Bible reading notes, and this forms a basis for informal discussion. She often initiates the conversation.

Children also take note of *how* we pray. Do we keep a prayer journal? Do we have a 'prayer buddy', or are we part of a prayer triplet or prayer group? Do we have others praying for us and our family? Do they ever see us going forward for prayer ministry in church? Do they see us praying with others? This may affect how much they participate in prayer themselves, both at home and in church.

If your children have not grown up with prayer as a natural part of their lives, don't worry! They will still be watching and learning from you. Your role will always be to encourage them and to be there for them, but, as they mature, they do need to feel that they have choices. Again, Bible reading notes can be the help they need. If they don't want to use these, one of the ideas in this book may help.

Young teens will be affected by their peers. We have seen one of our fourteen-year-old daughter's friends come to faith through our daughter's prayers. They became prayer buddies and started meeting weekly for prayer and Bible study. Now they are joined by other friends from their youth group for Bible study on another night in the week. They are all being challenged by each other's prayer lives.

Sunday groups

You may find that praying in groups on a Sunday is a relaxed affair, with the children eager to pray, but it can be more of a challenge if the children find this difficult or embarrassing. The age of the children and how accustomed they are to praying together will affect their response. Writing or drawing their prayers can be the answer for children who find it hard to pray out loud. For those who can't sit for very long, an active prayer time using prayer games, drama, dance or singing may help. Using music as a prayer focus can calm children and provide the prayer time with a beginning and an end. Similarly, candles can be used. During a time of listening to God, the children may like to write or draw what comes into their minds so that they don't later forget.

The Lord does speak to children. The question is: Do we take what they say seriously? We had a four-year-old boy at the New Wine Conference a few years ago whose parents told us that he regularly had words which were received by his church. The Lord asks us to come as little children. We can learn a lot from their trust and faith.

Children can pray together. We have successfully had children of five to twelve years old praying in groups together. We had already taught the older children about praying in a group. They would find out about the prayer needs of others in the group and pray for these. If it was for healing, they would lay hands on the child being prayed for. They would have times of listening to God, where they would write down what came into their mind while they were praying. This they would weigh, asking God which situation or person the word was intended for, and checking whether this was from God or something God wanted shared. They would share this with their Sunday group leaders. As they grew in experience, we used the older children to show the younger ones how to pray by doing it with them. In this way they modelled prayer. This also served the purpose of helping to develop leadership skills in the older children.

School assembly

Schools work is beyond the scope of this book, except to say
that unless the school is a Christian school, care needs to be
taken to protect the integrity of the children in the school
assembly. Some of the children may be practising in other
faiths and this we are bound to recognise and respect. Others
may not have a faith or be from families that are atheist. The
children should not be placed in a position where they are
asked to pray or sing anything they cannot mean.

We can tell them what the Bible says or what Christians
believe. We can tell them that Christians talk to God and
that this is what we will do now. We can invite them to listen
to the prayer and if they agree with what we are saying,
they can say 'Amen' at the end. As we pray, we should avoid
phrases and sentiments that will exclude some children –
for example, telling Jesus how much we love him.

A useful book for work in schools is *The Schools Work
Handbook* by Emlyn Williams (Scripture Union).

Praying in church

It is possible to pray creatively in church. Churches that use
the *Scripture Union SALT All-Age* or similar material may
be used to the idea of different ways of praying. For those
who are not, and for those who are but need a longer time
than the church services permit, it may be possible to introduce prayer on other occasions.

We have a special service in our church on Maundy
Thursday and this has been a good day for us to experiment, especially with ideas which require more space, like
a parachute or playchute, and activities like painting,
model-making or writing prayer poems, which may require
more time. We have also found that these occasions have
been good for longer times of quiet reflection. The Lord has

so blessed us that children have been reluctant to go home – they have not wanted to leave the presence of the Lord. An example of this is given in Prayer Idea 95.

Children and spiritual gifts

The promise of the Holy Spirit is for all people who believe and trust in Jesus, including children: 'Repent and be baptised, every one of you, in the name of Jesus Christ for the forgiveness of your sins. And you will receive the gift of the Holy Spirit. The promise is for you and your children and for all who are far off – for all whom the Lord our God will call' (Acts 2: 38–39, NIV). We see in the Scriptures that God uses children (e.g. Samuel, David, Naaman's servant girl, Mary the mother of Jesus) and in our own experience at conferences, in church and at home we have witnessed God using children who are willing and available to him to use.

In 1990 God gave a word to our church that he would fill our children with his Holy Spirit. The question was: How do we get from where we are now to children exercising spiritual gifts? Our Sunday school at the time was quite traditional. After attending the New Wine Conference, we were inspired by the approach of Captain Alan Price, as he led the Captain's Crew children's team. God had told us that we would find the key to our own situation here, and we did. We had to go for it! As Children's Ministry Coordinator, I shared this with my vicar, who was supportive. Confirmation that we were hearing God came through a visiting speaker, Mart Vahi, from Estonia. The next step was to tell the church and then the children!

It was three weeks before our children in the seven to thirteen age range could believe that God would use them. These children had grown up in the church and had a relationship with Jesus. After three weeks, we began to teach them about the gifts of the Holy Spirit. We found Richard

Hubbard's book, *Taking Children Seriously* (Marshall Pickering), an excellent resource, as was Ishmael's *Angels with Dirty Faces* (Kingsway).

We witnessed the power of God at work through the children, and so did they. This was faith-building for all of us. The children learned about weighing what was said alongside seeing other children healed as a result of their prayers. They learned about being channels for God. They also learned that the healing may not come as they had hoped but that the child receiving prayer was feeling the presence of God and this brought blessing.

During this time, we were learning as leaders. We worked closely with our vicar, we read the Scriptures, we sought the Lord and we delighted in the children. They wanted to be used by God and God was responding. We may not have done everything by the book – if there is a book to follow! – but God knew that we were seeking to move responsibly. As well as gifting the children, we were aware of God's purpose in character development. Our lives speak to others. What are others seeing in our lives? Do they see the fruit of the Spirit? The fruit and the gifts go together.

It is beyond the scope of this book to examine spiritual gifts in depth, but some of the ideas in this book do make reference to laying on of hands or to hearing the Lord speak. When children don't know how to pray, they can pray in their own prayer language. This deepens their relationship with God.

All of us need to be constantly filled and refilled with the Spirit of God. We need to confess our wrong actions, our wrong words, our wrong attitudes. We need to know the word of God, and this will give us confidence as we pray because then we are more able to pray in accordance with God's will.

God will use children. He will use them now. Enjoy praying with your children.

PART TWO

SECTION 1: FAMILY LIFE

As for my family and me, we will serve the Lord. (Joshua 24:15)

The family is the place where our experiences of being alive begin. The ways we feel about ourselves, about other people, about the world in which we live, are affected by these early experiences. Our needs are met within the family – needs for food, warmth, close contact, a place of safety and feeling valued.

The family is the natural place for us to learn to talk with our Father God. It is the place to learn to love and care for others, to reach out to the wider world under the protection of our parents. It is the place for developing relationships God's way.

Our families are made up of adults and children, covering a variety of ages, together experiencing the same home environment. Both in our home and church, we have seen how younger children learn from the praying of older children, as well as from the praying of their parents and other adults in their lives. For a while in our church, we deliberately had older children model prayer for younger children, and this was a very rich experience for all concerned.

The prayer ideas that follow have children of all ages in

mind. The ideas progress to offer greater challenges for the older child, but can be used with children across the age range with consideration for the abilities and stage of development of each individual and family.

1. Family fun times

Family fun times are about all the things families do together and enjoy. This may be playing games in the park like tennis over a log or football with trees marking the goalposts; baking cakes; outings to the cinema; visiting a safari park; going to the beach or leisure centre; holidays; walks; cycle rides; planting the children's own spot in the garden; playing board games . . . the list is endless!

These can all provide opportunities for praying together. You may not want to use everything you do as a family as a basis for prayer, although the events of the day will often quite naturally come to mind if you pray with children at bedtime. If there are breathtaking moments while you are out, it may be the time to marvel at all that

God has made. You may be challenged to pray for something you see as you travel along the road, or you may be reminded of the plight of others as you walk through a city centre. You may be moved as you stand in the slightly esoteric atmosphere of a cave house. All these experiences can lead into prayer.

What you need

A willingness to talk together and to include God in those conversations

Using the idea

With younger children you could say, 'Let's thank God for the fun we have had today.'

Each member of the family could think of one thing they would like to say 'thank you' to God for from the events of the day. You may want to do this over a mealtime or at bedtime. The children's prayers may go something like this:

Thank you, God, for the sunshine (the bike ride, the swim, the trip to the park, the walk in the wood, the paddle in the sea, etc.).

Father God, thank you that we could go to the park today. I like riding my bike and playing on the slide. I like feeding the ducks too. Amen.

Dear Lord, thank you that I can swim. I like going to the swimming pool. I especially like the leisure pool and swimming in the rapids. Amen.

Lord Jesus, thank you for the places we can see when we've climbed to the top of the hills. Is that a bit like

when you look across the earth? You like the earth you have made and I like it too. Amen.

Heavenly Father, thank you for my family. I like holidays when we can do so many fun things together. Amen.

While out on a walk you may want to express appreciation to God as you look at the view, examine a leaf, or marvel at the blossom on the tree or the complexity of a flower. This can be taken as far as the interest of the children will allow. It is about appreciating what God has made as you talk together and then letting this lead on to telling God how much you marvel at his creativity.

With older children, we've marvelled in caves at the stalactites and stalagmites, the hidden pools and streams, the underground water courses that cut through the rock in the first place – a world hidden until one day cavers or miners discovered it, but a world that is part of God's creation and a reminder of what God is doing in us in the inner parts of our beings as we yield to him.

We have stood inside disused cave houses and prayed for the homeless, for those living without running water in their homes, for those struggling to care for their families, especially in countries where there is no state help, but also in this country when children can find it hard in the competitive world of school, friendships and materialism.

Using family times to talk can lead to children sharing more of themselves with their parents and vice versa. These are bonding times. They are also times that bring great reward as the children's joys and concerns are shared and offered in prayer.

Song

Your face is full of wonder (*SOFK*)

2. Is something worrying you?

Even good things that happen to our children can cause them to worry. A child doing really well with swimming can become anxious when taking a swimming badge. Children may worry about starting pre-school or a new school. Going to the doctors or the dentist may be stressful, especially if the child's experience of going in the past has not been good. Whatever our age, there are things that we don't like doing but have to do.

There may be worries that affect the whole family, like illness, redundancy or unemployment. These may have an impact on lifestyle. In the case of illness, it may affect the workload on other members of the family and, in addition, there may be coping with visits to hospital and worries about whether or not the person will recover. Unemployment and redundancy have an effect on the money available to the family and therefore may affect pocket money.

Without wanting to create worries where there are none, children can be encouraged to talk over anything that causes them concern about any situation affecting the family or themselves. Any member of the family might value prayer support at these times and even young children can be praying for their parents or brothers and sisters.

What you need

Awareness of the child's response to an event or situation

Using the idea

This can be as a whole family praying together for the particular need, or it can be more informal, with you praying with the child or the child praying for you. The children can pray for each other. It can be a shared need that members of the family pray for on their own. How this develops may depend upon the praying relationship that you already have as a family. If the child is suffering a lot of trauma, outside help may be required.

One way of praying for each other which is used in our church is to pray fear, shock and trauma off one another. The trauma of daily life is enough in itself! Maybe the child has fallen over, had an operation or experienced a fright, so you could pray:

> *I pray off the fear, shock and upset (trauma) in the name of Jesus. I ask you, Lord Jesus, to take this away and to fill [name] with your Holy Spirit. Amen.*

Children can be taught to pray this over you or other family members. It may help them to know that, after this prayer, the person being prayed for may begin to cry, shake, sigh or breathe heavily. Tell the children not to worry if this happens as this is the body's way of letting go of the trauma. You could explain that when something bad happens to us our bodies often tense up and the upset (or the trauma) becomes locked up inside the body and, after a length of time, in the mind. As we pray, the Holy Spirit relaxes the body and the crying, shaking, sighing or heavy breathing is the trauma lifting. Not everyone responds in this way, of course, so it is perfectly all right if the person being prayed for shows no outward sign!

Another way of praying is to give the concern to the Lord.

Father God, you have told us to bring to you all our worries. I want to do that with this worry. I am worried about the football match on Wednesday. I really want to play well and not let the team down. I need your help. In Jesus' name. Amen.

Dear Lord, we are really worried about Mum. She is in so much pain. Help her to get the pain relief that she needs and help us to know how best to help her. We are sad because she has broken her arm. Please be with us too and help us not to be more worried than we need to be. Thank you. In Jesus' name we pray. Amen.

Songs

Do not worry (*SOFK*)
Father, I place into Your hands (*JP*)
I once was frightened (*SOFK*)

3. Praying for healing

It is good for children to be included in praying for others when they are ill, and what better place to be doing this than in the family? This doesn't need to take long – in fact it is unlikely to with lively young children! Older children are learning more about ministering in prayer as they pray like this in the family. This idea encourages the following of the scriptural practice of prayer with the laying on of hands, but praying for others does not need to include this.

What you need

A willingness for the children to pray with the laying on of hands

Using the idea

If you have been praying with the laying on of hands in your family since the children were born, then no explanation will be required.

If this is a new idea, explain that God is a God who can heal and that he can do it through them. Tell them that one way God uses to heal us is when other people pray and place their hands on us. Maybe they will have seen this in your church. Ask them if they would like to do this for you or whoever it is in your family who is not well.

To help them, suggest that they place one hand gently on the person (maybe on their shoulder) and hold their other hand up towards God. This will help to remind them that it is God who does the healing. He uses them as a channel of his love and healing.

You may need to help them to say a prayer to begin with, but as this becomes a more natural part of family life, then the children will become more confident about praying themselves. The prayer might go something like this:

Father God, we ask you to bring your healing to [name] in the name of Jesus. Holy Spirit, come and touch him through us. May he feel you now deep within him. May he know your love and care. Come, Holy Spirit.

You can stay with this for as long as you feel everyone is comfortable. The children can pray in tongues if this is in their experience. Then conclude with something like:

Thank you, Lord Jesus. Amen.

Younger children will not want to spend long on this. Their own prayer is most likely to be a short sentence. This was the case with a three-year-old called Emma. Her mum had been making the beds when she winded herself while stretching across the top bunk. She was finding it difficult to breathe and had tensed up, which resulted in making her breathing worse. At that moment Emma needed the toilet. Her mum went with her and while she was sitting on the toilet, Emma asked her mum what was the matter. Her mum told her and said that she needed Jesus to help her. She asked Emma to pray. Still sitting on the toilet, Emma layed hands on her mum by giving her a big hug and said: 'Amen. Please, Jesus, help Mummy feel better.' Within thirty seconds her mum was able to breathe. Emma prayed from her heart because she loves her mummy and she was certain that Jesus would help. God will use the prayers of even the youngest child.

This way of praying can be used with any member of the family (including the cat, the dog or the rabbit) who is not feeling very well, and you may see younger children laying hands on their dolls or teddies.

We know that we are not always healed in the way we would like. This is our experience in prayer and it may well be the children's experience too. We need to reassure them that God has heard. We can always ask the person how they are, and often we will find that the Lord has touched them. They can testify to a blessing from the Lord, even if their healing is not so apparent. We can thank God for this blessing.

ADDITIONAL IDEA

It can be difficult for a young child to pray for others because their life revolves around themselves, but by gathering children together at home you can ask them to say one thing for which they would like prayer. Brothers and sisters can join in praying about this. Take turns and include yourself.

4. Photographs

This is a good way of praying for family members or friends who are away from home or live further away. The photographs can bring back good memories of times together, and for these we can thank God.

What you need

Photographs of family members, or the family photograph album

Using the idea

(i) Use the photographs to bring to mind the person to be

prayed for.

(ii) Talk about that person, share together any needs you know they have and use these for prayer. For example:

> *Lord, please be with our cousin John as he takes his exams. Help him to stay calm and to remember what he has revised. Thank you, Jesus. Amen.*

ADDITIONAL IDEA

Make a prayer photograph album

What you need

A photograph album or scrapbook
OR
Stiff paper or card
Slide binder, or string or wool and a hole-punch
Photograph corners or glue stick

Using the idea

Attach the stiff paper or card together using the slide binder or by punching holes and tying together with string or wool passed through the holes.

Place the photographs of family and friends in your prayer photograph album. Depending on how many people you want to include, allocate a day in the week/month/year when you will pray together for them. You may want to label the pages with these dates and the names of the people on the photographs. This activity can be daily or weekly and planned accordingly.

Use the photographs to bring to mind the person being prayed for. Talk about the person, share together any needs you know they have. These people may be at home in the family (in which case you can ask them what they would like you to pray about), living close by or living away.

Song

Your face is full of wonder (*SOFK*)

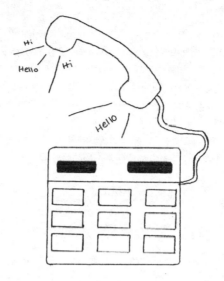

5. Using the telephone

This often happens naturally with family members who are not with us at home. If Mum or Dad has to go away, they usually ring. We keep in touch with grandparents and uncles and aunts in the same way. A telephone call can provide an opportunity to talk to God, either after the telephone has been put down, or during the call, praying for the person over the telephone.

What you need

A telephone

Using the idea

The telephone conversation will have helped the children
to think again about these people and it may have given
them some suggestions for prayer. Our thoughts are with
them and, if this is a close family member, the children may
well be missing them. This is a good time for them to tell
God how they feel.

I'm sad, Lord, I didn't want them to go.

Or the emotion might be anger:

I'm cross, Lord. I want them to be here with me.

As we listen to the children, we can help them to give their
feelings to the Lord and we can ask God to minister his
comfort to the children.

*Lord Jesus, please be with [name] in his sadness, and
help him to know that Dad loves him and cares for him
and will be home [tomorrow]. Amen.*

We need an expectation that the children will be touched
by the Lord. They often receive comfort in knowing that, as
God is with them, so he is with the one who is away.

The child may be quite all right about Dad being away
and the prayer might be:

*Father God, please be close to Dad tonight and help
him to know that you are with him. Keep him safe as he
travels home.*

ADDITIONAL IDEA

Praying over the telephone

Encourage the child to pray for the family member over the telephone. How readily a child will do this depends on the individual and how comfortable they are about praying and especially about praying with the person on the telephone. A small child might pray:

> *Please, Lord Jesus, make Mummy better. Amen.*

An older child might say:

> *Dear Lord, I pray for Mum. Help her operation to go well and be successful. Help her not to be too anxious. Help her to recover quickly. Thank you, Lord. Amen.*

If the child needs prayer, they could receive the prayer over the telephone. Talk about how useful telephones are and what a wonderful means this is for praying for someone who cannot be with you at the moment. We can receive the words spoken and they encourage us. The contact reflects God's love and care for us shown through other people.

Praying over the telephone is also referred to in Section 3: Friends.

Song

Prayer is like a telephone (*SOFK*)

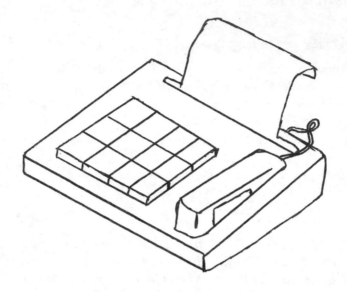

6. Long-distance prayer

Older children will enjoy the challenge of electronic communication – communication being the key here. The objective is to keep in touch, to show we care and also to help us know better how to pray. You can do this using fax, which is a good way of keeping in touch and sending children's drawings, early writing, etc. to family members living away.

What you need

Access to a fax machine, both for yourself as the sender and for the person receiving the fax

Using the idea

The fax provides the information for prayer. The whole family can be together while the fax is sent and the reply received, or if it happens at a time when the family is not together, it can be used at family prayer time, family meal-times or children's bedtimes. This depends a little bit on the prayer routine of your family.

ADDITIONAL IDEAS

E-mail

If you have access to E-mail, this is also a very good way of keeping in touch, especially with family members who live overseas, as up-to-date news is passed on quickly and cheaply.

The Internet

Visiting websites on the Internet may not be praying for family members but it involves the children in finding out information for praying for others at family prayer times. Many organisations have websites on the Internet and visiting these can give up-to-date prayer news. (See Part Three for some website addresses.)

7. Prayer drawing

If children find speaking prayers aloud difficult, get them to draw their prayer. They don't need to speak their prayer drawing, but if they want to talk to you about it, you can be there to listen. This idea works well at an all-age service in church too.

What you need

Paper, pencils, crayons; or dry-wipe board and appropriate pens

Using the idea

With younger children, you might like to cut out a particular shape for the prayer picture. For example:

- If Dad has gone away for the night on a train, bus or plane, the paper could be train-, bus- or plane-shaped.
- If Mum is in hospital, it could be hospital-shaped.
- If an older brother or sister is camping, it could be tent-shaped.
- If Nanny and Grandad have just moved house, it could be house-shaped.

Older children are good at making their own shapes, but they may prefer to write their prayers.

ADDITIONAL IDEAS

Writing prayers

Writing prayers down helps many children to have the confidence to pray out loud. It is not necessary for written prayers to be spoken, but this can help children to overcome their shyness of praying out loud. Some children may want to write and draw their prayers.

What you need

Paper (can be cut into shapes)
Pens or pencils

Using the idea

This can be used as part of a family prayers activity or at

bedtime. The prayer could be written onto an aeroplane shape and flown across the room. Someone else in the family could pick it up and pray it out loud.

Displaying prayers

Prayers can be displayed on a prayer board.

What you need

Pinboard, hardboard or thick card
Drawing-pins or glue stick
Prayer drawings or written prayers

Using the idea

Attach the pictures or written prayers to the prayer board as part of each person's praying of the prayers. This can be done together at a family prayer time or as the children draw or write them.

8. Making cards

These can be sent to the person you are praying for (e.g. nanny, grandad, aunty, uncle, brother, sister, mum, dad) to let them know that they are in your prayers.

What you need

Card, crayons, felt-pens
Glue, cut-out pictures, pressed flowers, pasta, stickers, glitter, etc. (optional)

Using the idea

Making the card will help the child to think about the

person concerned. Talk about why you are making the card (Get Well, Birthday, Congratulations, New Baby) and allow this conversation to lead on naturally to praying for the person.

Heavenly Father, this card is for Nanny. When she opens it, let her have an even happier birthday. Thank you, Lord. Amen.

The child could write a message inside the card telling the person that they are praying for them. For example: 'Just to let you know I'm praying for you and I love you lots' or: 'I'm asking Jesus to make you better'.

9. Prayer biscuits

Gifts could be made instead of cards. One idea is biscuits.

What you need

Your favourite biscuit recipe
OR
150g (6oz) self-raising flour
Half a teaspoon of bicarbonate of soda
100g (4oz) sugar
100g (4oz) margarine
1 egg
1 tablespoon warm golden sugar (optional)
Bowl, spoon, baking tray

To make the biscuits

1. Wash hands.
2. Mix all dry ingredients together.
3. Rub in margarine.
4. Add egg and golden syrup.
5. Knead into soft dough.
6. Divide dough into small balls and flatten down on a greased baking tray with your hands. Alternatively, flatten down the dough on a floured board and use biscuit-cutters to cut out shapes (rabbits, cars, trains, etc.) and place on a greased baking tray.
7. Bake in a moderate oven (Gas mark 3–4; electric 300–350°F) for approximately ten minutes.
8. Gently lift the biscuits off the tray and leave to cool on a wire rack.
9. Once cool, they can be decorated with icing or they can be eaten as they are.

Using the idea

While making the biscuits, talk about the person you are making them for and bring God into the conversation. For example: 'We're making these biscuits for Grandma. Let's ask God to be with her.'

Arrange the biscuits on a plate and take them to the person they've been made for. If appropriate, the children could tell them that these are prayer biscuits and explain that they have been praying for them while making the biscuits. A hug would probably be a good ending for the prayer. The children could make an accompanying card saying: 'I'm praying for you!'

10. Happy families

What is your family like? Could it be described as happy?
What makes a happy family? Ephesians 5:22–33 talks
about how husbands and wives should be towards each
other and Ephesians 6:1–4 tells us how parents and children should be. Colossians 3:18–21 covers the same things.
The secret seems to be in love, forgiveness and each doing
their part.

What you need

Paper and pencil

Using the idea

Ask the children what they think Mum and Dad should do
for them (older children could write this down). Now ask
them what they think they should do for Mum and Dad. If
they already have jobs to do, are they happy to do them?
What about bedtimes, or keeping other house rules (like
taking your shoes off when you come home, hanging your
coat up, making your bed)? Think about the times when
everyone is happiest with everyone else. Is it when every-
body does their part? With older children, you could also
read Ephesians 5:22 – 6:4. A prayer might be:

> *Lord Jesus, help me to do the things I am asked to do*
> *willingly and cheerfully. Help me to remember to hang*
> *my coat up. I'm sorry I keep forgetting. Amen.*

The children could ask God to help them share readily in
the household tasks. If they are not already doing jobs, they
could think about what they would like to do. Washing-up
may not be their favourite activity, but dusting and polish-
ing may be a delight!

What about bedtimes? If this is a contentious issue, they
could ask God to help them to go to bed without being
told!

What about when someone is not doing their part?
When this is realised, they need to say 'sorry' (including
Mum and Dad!), and those who have been hurt or upset
need to forgive. If this is difficult to do, they can ask God to
help them.

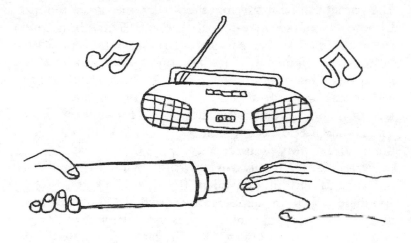

11. Pass the parcel

Children love to have fun, and games can capture their imagination. The traditional game of pass the parcel is popular with all ages, although very young children may not be quite so keen to pass the parcel on!

What you need

Something to wrap the parcel in
A prize for the middle
Prayers to go in between layers

Using the idea

The parcel can be made together or by one of the family. Choose a suitable prize to be wrapped – something that everyone can share, e.g. favourite biscuits, chocolate buttons, fruit, mini chocolate bars, or a note saying what it is if it is too big or not possible to wrap, such as an outing. The outing could be a visit to the park or cinema, a bike ride, or helping you with the shopping at the supermarket! The choice is endless and can be tailor-made to suit your family and dietary preferences.

Prayers for the family can be written by family members beforehand and interleaved in the wrappings or spoken spontaneously as the headings are revealed. (You could use photographs of family members instead, although not ones you want to keep looking nice as this game may cause them to crumple!)

The prayers may go like this:

Lord Jesus, please help [Ben] to play well in the football match tomorrow.

Please help [Louise] to remember her tables in the test tomorrow.

The game is played like the traditional game of pass the parcel, with the parcel being passed round the family while the music is playing. When the music stops, the person holding the parcel unwraps the layer and follows the instructions.

ADDITIONAL IDEAS

Pass the bowl/cup/mug/box

These are simply variations on the theme. Folded papers written on by the family are placed in the container. While the music plays, pass the container, and when the music stops, pray.

Other games

Most games can be adapted with imagination! What about hunt the thimble or a treasure hunt? Objects can be hidden in a room, garden or house. Suggestions include photographs (possibly in unbreakable frames), a favourite toy or something that will remind everyone else of who the object will be representing. Dare I suggest washing-up gloves for Mum, a screwdriver for Dad, a cuddly toy for the youngest – or are they all into computer games these days? Your family will have ideas!

12. Family prayer book

Keeping a family prayer book is another way of sharing prayer needs. Members of the family can write their prayer needs in the prayer book and other members can look at it to find out what to pray for.

What you need

An attractive book. You may want to get the children to help you choose the book. One with gold edges might appeal to your children, or one with coloured pages and plenty of space to write or draw. The picture on the cover might be more important to them. The objective is to find one that the children will want to use.

Using the idea

You may want to write down prayer requests for the next family prayer night, or you may want to pray each day for the events or concerns of the day. If you pray together at mealtimes, this might be the time.

If the children are older when you introduce this idea, they may prefer to pray for their parents, brothers and sisters in their own prayer times. Choosing the how and when may very much depend on the praying relationship you have together as a family. When prayers are answered, this can be recorded alongside the prayer request. A tick may be sufficient, or your children may want to write the date.

Song

As for me and my house (*SOFK*)

SECTION 2: SCHOOL LIFE

Always remember what you have been taught . . . (Proverbs 4:13, NCV)

Children spend a lot of time in school. It is a central part of their lives and it can be a joy and delight or it can be stressful, depending upon such things as the relationships they have and how well they feel they are coping with the work. We need to pray for them as well as encourage them to pray for their teachers, their friends, their work and the effect that other members of the school community can have on their lives.

The pressures of SATS begin very early in the children's school career. They need to know that they are valued for who they are and not just for what they produce. We need to affirm them and surround them with love, care and support.

13. School prayer club

Some schools have Christian groups for children. These may be an hour-long programme of activities, or groups meeting for fifteen minutes specifically for Bible study or prayer. They are voluntary and meet either before school, at lunchtime or after school, and are led by teachers, parents or someone from a local church.

What you need

Children who want to pray for their school

Using the idea

If there isn't already a group meeting in the school, the children could talk to a teacher about starting one. They do need supervision and some direction, so once the school has given permission, an adult needs to be found who can take responsibility for the group. Decide on a meeting time and the nature of the group, and publicise it. The children may want to choose a catchy name for it. The name chosen for our group was Power Pack.

Scripture Union in Schools is a helpful resource for running the group and if it is a prayer group, once they have the idea, the children themselves will be able to suggest topics for prayer, like money for equipment, problems like bullying, stealing and safety, and concerns such as exams and friendships that they will be aware of as children in the school.

14. The school day

God is with us wherever we are and we can talk to him at any time. He is the only friend who knows what we are saying when we talk to him in our heads. He shares our joys and our sorrows. He is concerned about all the things that concern us. This idea encourages children to talk to God anywhere and at any time, and knowing they can gives them security as they go to school. They know that they are not on their own. God is with them. If they need any encouragement about this, you could show them Joshua 1:9: 'Don't be afraid or discouraged, for I, the Lord your God, am with you wherever you go.'

What you need

A Bible (if required)

Using the idea

Tell the children that they can talk to God anywhere and at any time, and that that includes when at school. If they feel unhappy about something they can tell God. If they are nervous, frightened or worried they can tell God and ask him to draw close to them in a way that they can feel, and they can ask him to give them courage. If they feel alone in tests or exams they can tell God. They may feel so nervous that they need him to give them peace inside, which will help them to recall what they have learned. If they feel threatened in the playground or put down by a teacher they can place their hand in Jesus' hand. He is their big friend and he is with them.

Good things happen at school too and they can tell God about these things. They can thank him for a good test result; for being praised; for answering their prayer so that they are no longer worried or anxious or afraid about their team winning the game; for a school trip.

Thank you, Lord, that you are with me wherever I am.
I like that. Amen.

ADDITIONAL IDEA

Jesus is with you

To remind them that Jesus is with them wherever they are, the children could draw a picture of different places and write under it: 'Jesus is with me wherever I am.' They could put this up on their noticeboard. Another reminder is to draw a small picture of a cross and cut it out, or to make one out of two small twigs. This can be kept in the pocket. You may want to tell the children that this is not Jesus, so it doesn't matter if they haven't got it with them because it is only there to remind them of the truth that Jesus is with them wherever they are.

Songs

Do not worry (*SOFK*)
Great, great, brill, brill (*SOFK*)
I can do all things (*SOFK*)
I'm not alone (*SOFK*)
In our work and in our play (*JP*)
Now be strong and very courageous (*JP*)

15. Who's your teacher?

Teachers are very important to our children. They have a profound effect upon their happiness and learning while at school, and we need to pray for them in these days of added pressure.

What you need

Paper, pencil, crayons
Play-doh, clay or pipe-cleaners

Using the idea

Ask the children about their teachers. They may not like

the teacher they have at the moment, so you could talk about why they don't like them. Older children might like to think about all the different teachers they have had. What did they like most about their favourite teachers? How well do they think they learned? Why do they think this was?

Some children might like to draw a picture of their teacher. Others may like to make a model of their teacher using play-doh, clay or pipe-cleaners. The children could make a picture of all the teachers who teach them if they have more than one. These can be put onto a prayer board or into the children's prayer book. The children could write a list of the things that they would like to pray for their teacher and this can be put alongside the picture. They may also like to thank God for their teacher.

16. Odd one out

When we are new to something we can feel as if we are the odd one out. Did you ever move house as a child and have to start a new school? What did it feel like? Often children feel lonely and sad because they have left their friends behind, or anxious because they don't know anyone. This idea helps children to think about what it is like for children joining their class at school.

What you need

Several pairs of socks and one odd one

Using the idea

Get the children to sort and pair up the socks. When they have finished, they will find an odd one. Use this to talk about how it feels to be the odd one out – maybe because a child is new to the group or speaks with a different accent. The children could think about how they feel when someone new joins the class. Is it easy to make friends with them? What can make it difficult? The child may be frightened of the other children. Are the other children frightened of the new child? New children will find their own friends, but as they are doing this, perhaps they could be friendly towards them. The talking can lead on to praying:

Dear Lord, please be with [Joshua] and help him quickly to feel a part of our class. Help us all to be friendly towards him. Amen.

Lord Jesus, thank you that we know you are with us wherever we go. You are the best friend that we can have. Amen.

17. Where do we fit?

This prayer idea takes us into a wood or a forest where we can look at the levels in the vegetation. We look up to see the trees towering over our heads like a canopy. We look around to see the bushes and we look down beneath our feet to see the grass and the flowers covering the floor of the forest.

The canopy layer has a job to do. It protects the vegetation below and provides homes for many animals, birds and insects. Similarly, each of these other layers has a particular job to do in the forest and they are all dependent on each other. It is from considering this that this prayer idea has been inspired.

What you need

To go into a wood or forest

Using the idea

While enjoying your walk in the wood, stop from time to time to look at the trees and vegetation. Let the children tell you about what they can see – the tall trees, the bushes, the grass and flowers (roughly three layers). Ask the children how they feel standing under the tall trees. Do their feelings change as they stand on the grass?

The structure of the forest can be likened to the structure of the school. For example, the teachers are like the canopy layer, the children in the reception class are like the vegetation near the ground and the children in the top class are like the taller bushes. This could lead on to discussing how the children feel about being with those older and younger, and the responsibilities that come with each position in the school. The canopy layer in the wood protects the layers below. Pray that those in authority in the school will care for those who are younger and that each person will take responsibility for their own place within the school. This will include respecting those who are bigger and caring for those who are smaller.

Dear Lord, please help our school to be a caring school. Amen.

Lord Jesus, we want to be happy at school. Help us to watch out for each other, especially those who are younger than we are who may be picked on. Help our teachers to be fair. Amen.

ADDITIONAL IDEA

This idea could also be used to pray for our country. The layers could represent those in authority at the top, to those without much status at the bottom. The children could pray for the Queen, the prime minister or the government at the top and the homeless at the bottom. The same feelings can be explored for each group and their responsibilities considered.

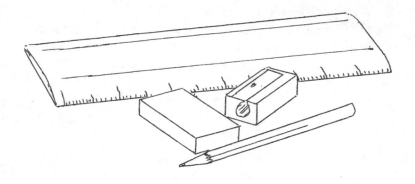

18. Symbols of school

When you think about school, what thoughts come into
your mind? Is it the uniform, carrying lots of things to
school, broken or blunt pencils, lessons, school dinners?
This idea takes objects that are associated with school and
uses them to help the children to pray for their school, their
lessons and their teachers.

What you need

An assortment of objects that are associated with school

Using the idea

Display the objects you have collected, for example pen, pencil, ruler, rubber, exercise book, text book, reading book, PE kit, musical instrument, school bag, dinner money, school lunch. Ask the children to choose one and to think about it. What thoughts come into their mind? Use these thoughts to pray about school. For example:

- *Musical instrument*: Dear Lord, thank you that I can play this musical instrument well. Amen.
- *Rubber*: Thank you that I can rub out my mistakes with my rubber. Amen.
- *Pencil*: Thank you that I can draw pictures with my pencil. Amen.
- *Maths book*: Lord, I find maths hard. Please help me to learn and to do my best. Amen.
- *School bag*: This makes me think of school. I don't always want to go, but thank you that there is a school for me to go to and that I do enjoy it when I'm there because I'm with my friends. Amen.

Songs

God rubbered out all my mistakes (*SOFK*)
The Calculator Song (*SOFK*)

19. Penfriends

Do you remember ever having a penfriend? I had one in England, one in France (to help me to learn French!) and, later, one in Sweden. Some schools are twinned and everyone in the class has a penfriend. Time is therefore given at school to write to them. Some children will be involved in aid programmes overseas and, as a class lesson, will write to their sponsors. If you sponsor a child overseas, your children can write letters to enclose with yours.

What you need

Writing paper, pen, stamp
A penfriend

Using the idea

You may first need to find a penfriend. Many children's magazines have penfriend pages. Suggest that the children look through these and find someone of a similar age with similar interests. One of our girls advertised through a flute playing magazine and had four children write back, all Christians with an interest in the flute. Another way of finding a penfriend is for the child to write to a missionary child and ask them if they would like to write to them. Missionaries linked to your church might be able to help with this.

Once the children have found a penfriend, they can write about themselves, their school, the area in which they live, their hobbies, pets and other interests. They can write about church if they want to. They can find out about their penfriend and what their school is like. If their penfriend is a Christian, they could ask if there is anything their penfriend would like them to pray about. If they are not Christians, the children can still pray. They can use what has been said in the letters for prayer.

ADDITIONAL IDEAS

E-mail

This is the cheapest way to keep in touch with friends at home and overseas, and is also the quickest. Most children enjoy using computers and may well prefer to E-mail their penfriends. If they do have a prayer relationship with their penfriends this can also be a speedy way of securing prayer support. The children can take their penfriend's delights or concerns and use these as they pray.

Look at the letters in the Bible

Tell the children how the apostles wrote to people to encourage them in their faith. They often included prayers in their letters (for examples see Paul's greetings and prayers in chapter 1 of Ephesians, Colossians, Philippians, Thessalonians, and his blessings at the ends). These prayers may give the children ideas for praying for their own friends. They could also pray these scriptures for their friends.

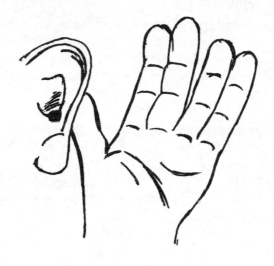

20. What did you say?

How do the children talk to their friends at school? Do they use the language of the school playground? They may want to because they don't want to be seen to be different. What about behaviour? Will they follow the crowd, or will they stand up for what they believe is right? It is not always easy to do the right thing if they are one of the gang.

What you need

Bibles (if required)

Using the idea

There may be a particular child who is causing concern for the children, or the issue could arise in a family or church group discussion. If the concern is with the behaviour of a particular child, talk it over and pray for that child.

If it is more general, you could ask the children to consider how they feel about other children telling lies, cheating with their work, stealing, hitting other children, telling tales or saying horrible things, and to think about what they can do. You could look with them at selected verses from Ephesians 4:17 – 5:1. This could lead on to praying in general or for particular children who come to mind. It could also lead to praying for strength not to be drawn into this way of speaking or behaving.

Song

Do what you know is right (*SOFK*)

21. Saying 'no'

What happens at school if the children are asked to do something they know is wrong? What about if they are on their way to school and someone they don't know offers them a sweet or a lift? Can they say 'no' and how do they do it? Do they shout it? Yes, in some situations. If someone is doing something to them that they don't like, they can shout to draw attention to the fact. Do they say 'no' firmly? Yes, if they are being badgered into doing something they know is wrong. Do they say 'no' politely? Yes, if they are being offered something they don't like.

What you need

Some role-play scenarios
Pens or pencils, paper

Using the idea

These are two ways of using this idea.

Role play

In pairs the children could practise saying 'no' in different ways. Offer some scenarios. For example: 'The dinner lady wants to give you more potato, but you have enough on your plate,' or, 'A child wants you to hit another child in the school playground.'

Do you say 'no' firmly, quietly, by shouting, with a smile or without a smile? Think about what messages are being given each time. Which is best for the situation?

This may lead on to talking about other ways of saying 'no' like:

- Choosing friends who think like they do.
- Avoiding certain situations by staying away from people who cause them a problem.
- Changing the subject.
- Ignoring the person.
- Speaking positive thoughts to themselves in their head.
- Sticking to a simple reply like: 'No, I don't want to.'

This can lead in to asking for God's help:

> *Lord Jesus, please help me to have the courage to say 'no' when I know something is wrong. Help me to know how to say 'no' and help me not to feel put down by*

other children when I don't want to do what they say. Amen.

Make a list

Do this individually, in pairs or all together. Ask the children to write down times when they should say 'no'. (*Note*: Younger children may need help in understanding that just because they don't want to do something this doesn't mean they can say 'no'. If the teacher wants them to go to assembly, they have to go. This is obedience.)

When they have done this, the children can ask God to help them to say 'no'.

Dear Lord, thank you that you have given us choices and that we can think about whether or not it is right to do something. When we know it is not, please help us to say 'no'. Amen.

Songs

Be bold (*JP*)
I'm gonna walk by faith (*SOFK*)
I'm not alone (*SOFK*)

SECTION 3: FRIENDS

Some friends may ruin you, but a real friend will be more loyal than a brother. (Proverbs 18:24, NCV)

Friends add so much to our lives. They enable us to see ourselves more positively. They encourage us. They challenge us. They understand us. Our lives are so much richer because of them and we would not want to be without them. Letting our friends know how much we appreciate them and care for them is our way of thanking them for their commitment to us.

A healthy friendship is a two-way relationship of loving and caring, sharing, giving and taking, being there and knowing they are there, standing up for each other. For children it is sitting together in school, playing together at playtime, walking home together, going to each other's birthday party, sharing secrets – and it can be reading the Bible and praying together.

Whether or not the latter becomes reality, the children are learning to trust and be trusted, to think about others and their needs, to be kind. They are learning about relationships and from them they are also learning about what it means to have a relationship with God; talking to him and sharing with him in the way they would with a friend. They learn that he is always there and that his is the best of friendships.

22. Trusting game

How far can you trust your friend? This game will help the children to find out!

What you need

A space big enough for the children to play the game safely
Blindfolds (optional)
Obstacle course (optional)

Using the idea

Divide the children into pairs and blindfold one of each pair. If preferred they could close their eyes, as not all children like blindfolds. Have the other child lead them around the room without bumping into anything. The leading child can do this by taking the blindfolded child's hand, or by having the blindfolded child place their right hand on the leader's left shoulder, or by talking to the blindfolded child and telling them where it is safe to go. Begin by walking, but then suggest they run (remind the leading child that they need to decide when it is safe to do this, as they are not to bump into anyone!).

Change over and then talk to the children about how it felt to be (a) the blindfolded child, and (b) the leading child.

They may come out with comments like: 'To begin with it was scary, but then it became easier as I felt more confident with their leading or directions,' or, 'It was harder when we started to run,' or, 'When I was leading I felt really responsible.'

The idea of this game is to lead on to praying about friendship. You could talk about how children make friends. Is the trust game a bit like that? To begin with the children were more cautious, their confidence growing as they experienced being cared for (or not!) by the leader. If they felt safe they would be more confident. If they were allowed to bump into things, they would stop trusting and become more cautious. The children could be asked what they were thinking about as they played the game. They may come up with questions like: How far can I trust this person? Will they be my friend when things get harder? How much can I tell them? Will they tell other people things that I have said to them in confidence?

Talk about this, then ask the children to think about whether they are a good friend. Did you care for the person you were leading, or did you let them bump into something? Do you stick up for your friends? Do you care for them? Do you share your toys, games, books, sweets with them? Do you keep secrets?

Let's thank God for our friends and ask him to help us to be better friends. For example:

Lord Jesus, thank you for my friends. My best friend is [Bethany] and [she] is always there for me. We sit on the bench at school together at playtime and kick our feet about. We sit next to each other in class and we're partners when we go on trips. I'm glad I've got [Bethany], as I feel safe. I know I won't be lonely and I won't feel left out. It's hard on the days when [she's] away, but I usually find someone to play with. Thank you, Lord, for my friends. Amen.

Dear Lord, please help me to be a better friend. Help me to think about the things my friends enjoy doing and not always to want them to do things my way. I want my friends to be able to trust me too. Help me not to tell other children what my friends only want me to know. Amen.

Obstacle course

Set up an obstacle course for the children to lead their partners safely across. This provides a greater challenge suitable for older children!

23. Prayer buddies

Being a prayer buddy is about praying together with a friend. This may begin by meeting together for Bible reading and, as the children learn to trust each other and become more confident in praying out loud with each other, they can begin to pray for each other.

What you need

A good friend willing to do this with you

Using the idea

One way to do this is to set a regular time each week to

meet together. After the preliminary chat, read from the Bible. One of our girls used the Bible reading plan at the front of her Bible as a way of getting started. You could use daily Bible reading notes and share with each other what you have been learning during the week. Having read the Scriptures and talked about God, start to think over what you would like to talk to God about. This may begin by using the prayer ideas in the Bible reading notes, or by praying for school, church or other friends. Over time, as confidence in each other grows, praying for more personal needs may develop and then the prayer support relationship begins which as the children move into their teenage years can be invaluable for them. The children are also learning about confidentiality and how to trust.

ADDITIONAL IDEA

Prayer triplets

Prayer triplets can meet together in a similar way to pray for a particular interest – for example, school or an overseas project.

24. What can I pray?

We all need prayer, but how good are we at asking for it? This idea is to help children to build up a praying relationship with their friends.

What you need

A piece of card and a pen

Using the idea

The children ask a friend to write down their prayer need on the card. This could be something they are happy about and want to give thanks for, or it may be something they are worried about, like a test at school. They then put the card in a place where it will be seen (in a Bible, on a noticeboard) as a reminder to pray. If the prayer need is for something in the future, they should ask the friend to let them know when it has been answered, and how, so they can stop praying or change the prayer.

25. Prayer chains

Talk to the children about supporting one another in prayer. One way of doing this is to form a prayer chain. This may be by telephone, but as this can be expensive another way is to have a prayer board in your group's meeting room. The objective is to encourage the children to allow others to pray for them, because we all need the prayers of others.

What you need

Pinboard or other suitable board
Mapping pins or similar
Pieces of paper

Notebooks for the children (optional)
Pens, pencils

Using the idea

Divide the board into two. On one half put the heading
'Lord we pray for . . .' and on the other half 'Thank you,
Lord, for answering our prayers'.

The children place their requests on the board and other
children who want to pray write down the prayer requests
in their prayer books or on a piece of paper. They take this
home with them to remind them to pray. The following
week, give time for the children to update the prayer board
by adding new prayers and by moving answered prayers
across to the 'thank you' side of the board.

ADDITIONAL IDEAS

Paper chains

Younger children may like to write their prayer requests on
slips of paper which could be linked to form a paper chain.
At the end of the session each child could take a link of the
chain home to remind them to pray.

People chains

Link arms to form a people chain. Everyone prays for the
next in line. At its simplest this prayer could be something
like:

Lord Jesus, please bless [Sam].

26. Prayer letters

This is especially good if the children have friends living some distance away. They can keep in touch by letter and, at the same time, write down their prayer needs.

What you need

Pen, writing paper, envelope, stamp

Using the idea

There are two ways of doing this. One is to write a newsy letter saying all that you have done and all you are planning to do, and the second way is to write down prayer topics for your friend to pray about. For example:

Joseph's Prayer Letter

Please pray for:
My SATS exams in May
A dental appointment on the 15th

We can thank God for:
Helping me to be brave
The sun shining on my birthday

Thank you for your prayers.

Your friend can do the same for you and in this way you can
support one another in prayer, keep up to date with news
and continue to develop your friendship.

ADDITIONAL IDEA

Write a letter to God

We often refer to Jesus as a friend, and children may like to
write to God or to Jesus, just as they might write to a friend,
to tell him how they are feeling. The children may need to
be told that it is all right to be honest with God. He can
handle it if we are angry or disappointed. He will still love
us, even if we are cross with him. He is the best of friends
and he has promised that he will not leave us (Deuteronomy 31:6). It may help the children to know that
people in the Bible were honest with God. They told him
how they were (e.g. David, Jonah, Job, Elijah, Hannah).

The children can also write happy, chatty letters to God
telling him all about their day. They may want to thank him
for the day and for being with them during it.

27. Saying 'sorry'

What happens when you fall out? Do you still want to be friends really? What can you do to make things right between you? The answer is in saying 'sorry', but this isn't an easy thing to do.

What you need

A willingness to make friends again

Using the idea

When children have fallen out with their friends they may need help to make friends again. This is a time when we can encourage them to pray for their friends; to thank God for the good times; to tell God that they are sorry they have fallen out and to ask him to help them to make up again; to tell God how they are feeling.

Lord Jesus, I really want us to be friends again but I'm scared. What if [Jade] doesn't want to be my friend any more?

I'm really sorry for the things I said, Lord. It's hard to say 'sorry'. Please help me.

I'm feeling hurt. I need to forgive, but it's hard. Please help me to forgive and help us to be friends again.

If the child feels it would help, they could take a present round to their friend's house when they say 'sorry', or they could invite them out – for example to the leisure centre for a swim.

28. What do I like about my friend?

You are friends, but why? What brought you together?
Why do you enjoy being together? What do you like doing
best together?

What you need

Paper and a pen

Using the idea

Write down all the things you like about your friend. For
example: sense of humour, good fun. Then write down what
a real friend helps you to do. For example: helps me when

I am sad, helps me when I'm hurt, plays with me when I'm lonely.

Then thank God for giving you such a good friend:

Dear Lord, thank you that [Gemma] is my friend and that [she] is good fun to be with. Thank you that [she] is a real friend by helping me when I'm sad and helping me when I'm hurt. Thank you that [she] plays with me when I'm lonely. Amen.

ADDITIONAL IDEA

Send your friend a card to thank them for being your friend.

Songs

Jesus is a friend of mine (*JP*)
Jesus is my friend (*SOFK*)

29. Birthday prayer album

It is important to remember our friends' birthdays, so why
not add photographs of them to your birthday book or
make a birthday prayer album?

What you need

Photographs of your friends
A birthday book or a photograph album to make into a
birthday prayer album

Using the idea

Find out your friends' birthdays, ask them for (or take!) a

photograph and place their pictures on the right birthday date. Make a special point of praying for them on their birthday. Don't forget to send them a card and/or present as well!

30. Friends in the Bible

There are many accounts of friends in the Bible. This idea looks at one of them: the healing of the paralysed man (Luke 5:17–26).

What you need

A Bible

Using the idea

Read the Bible passage, tell the story or sing the song 'Once there was a house' (by Ian White) and get the children to look at it from the point of view of the paralysed man and

103

his friends. Ask them to imagine they are one of the friends and then ask questions like:

- How do you feel when you arrive at the house and find that you can't get anywhere near Jesus?
- What are you thinking when you get onto the roof?
- How do you feel when Jesus heals your friend?
- What do you think when you see your friend walking?

Next, ask them to imagine they are the paralysed man.

- How do you feel when your friends come to get you and tell you that they are taking you to Jesus?
- What do you think when you see so many people in the house?
- How do you feel when your friends tell you that they are going to make a hole in the roof to get you to Jesus?
- How do you feel towards your friends when Jesus has healed you?

Then ask the children to pray as if they were the paralysed man or one of his friends. For example:

My Lord, you healed me! I'm so glad. What can I do to repay you? I am speechless. Thank you! Oh, thank you, my Lord. Bless my friends. They went to so much trouble to get me to you. Amen.

Dear Lord, I'm so happy! Thank you for healing my friend. I praise you, Lord. Amen.

Let this lead the children on to thanking God for their friends and the thoughtful things they do. They can also ask God to help them to be a good friend to their friends.

31. Paper people

The idea here is that the paper people represent the children's friends!

What you need

A rectangular piece of paper
Crayons or felt-pens
Scissors

Using the idea

Ask the children to think about their friends and then to choose three or four of them to pray for. Fold the piece of paper concertina-style to represent these friends, plus themselves. Draw a person on the top fold, with the hands and feet touching the side folds. Cut round the outline, leaving the hands and feet uncut. Open up and see the chain of people. Ask the children to write their own name on one of the people and the names of their friends on the others. Add a face, and colour in hair, clothes, etc. The children can look at this chain of friends as they pray for their friends.

The children could write Jesus' name on one of their people as a reminder that Jesus is their friend.

Song

Jesus is my friend (*SOFK*)

32. Being there

One of the best ways to show you are a good friend is to be there when your friend needs you: to sit by your friend in class, to play with your friend at playtime, to listen to your friend if they need to talk, to stick up for your friend. This is what being loyal is all about. Building with Lego bricks can illustrate this!

What you need

Lego bricks

Using the idea

Get the children to build something of their choice using the Lego. Look at what the children have made and talk about how each brick needs the one next to it to make it into a car or house or whatever the child has made. Liken this to how we need our friends. Our best friends are the ones we need most because they are the ones we do most things with. Point out that a Lego brick would miss the ones closest to it if they weren't there, as there would be nothing for it to be attached to. It's a bit like that with our best friends. We miss them when they are not at school because we are used to playing with them at playtime or sitting next to them in class. If they are not there we feel lonely and left out. God has given us friends to help us to grow into the people he wants us to be. Our friends help us to develop into caring and sharing people.

Encourage the children to be there for their friends. They could pray:

Lord God, please help me to be a good friend and to be there when my friends need me.

33. Sorry you're ill

Calling in on a friend who has not been at school is care in action, and praying for friends is all about caring. This idea is about showing the friend that someone is thinking about them, cares enough to call round and is praying for them.

What you need

A card or present (optional)

Using the idea

The children can call in to see their friend on the way home from school or, if the friend has a contagious illness or lives further away, they can chat on the telephone. This is cheering in itself. For longer-term conditions, making a card or taking a present shows care. The children could tell their friend that they are praying for them. If both are happy about praying together, they could pray with their friend. This can be done with the laying on of hands. Place one hand on or towards the friend and the other up towards God, as a reminder that it is God working through them. They then ask God to bring his healing. For example:

Father God, please heal [Andrew] in Jesus' name, and in the power of your Holy Spirit. Amen.

If the children are not praying with their friend, they can pray for them at home. Knowing they are being prayed for will have an effect on the friendship too. The sick friend may want to pray:

Thank you, Lord, that my friend cares enough about me to pray for me. Please bless [him]. Amen.

SECTION 4: MY NEIGHBOURHOOD

In your good pleasure make Zion prosper; build up the walls of Jerusalem. (Psalm 51:18, NIV)

Our neighbourhood is where we live. Older children may know their neighbourhood quite well, especially if they have lived there all their lives. They know the streets, the shops, the people. They know the way to school, and sooner or later are walking there by themselves.

Younger children enjoy going out to the park or helping with the shopping. These outings can provide an opportunity to talk to God about what they have seen and done during the day. Pretend play can help them to understand a little of what it is like to be doing the different jobs they come across. They can play at shops, doctors and nurses, libraries, schools, churches, post offices, swimming pools. (Yes, we played swimming pools! Our daughter's office play set became the pretend reception area of the leisure centre. We played at buying our tickets for swimming in the leisure pool or attending a gymnastics class.) When young children play these games it can give them ideas for prayers for the people in their town who are involved in jobs such as these.

Let us pray for our neighbourhood.

34. What's going on in your neighbourhood?

Finding out what's going on in your neighbourhood can give ideas for prayer. Local issues might be a project for your Sunday group, or it may be a particular family interest. These issues need not all be bad. Looking for good things in our area is important, as is remembering that our communities are made up of people, most of whom do care about others. Town councils usually have the best interests of their towns at heart!

What you need

Access to local news from newspapers, television, local radio, billboards, your public library

Notebook and pencil, tape recorder, video camera, questionnaire

The children's ideas

Using the idea

There are so many ways of using this idea because there are so many ideas! You may want to contrast the good things about living in your neighbourhood with the bad. You could display local issues for prayers of thanksgiving, and concerns for prayers of intercession or asking.

Articles could be cut out of newspapers and displayed on a prayer board or in a scrapbook with the prayers alongside. The overall heading could be 'Our neighbourhood', followed by a further two headings: 'Father God, thank you for all the good things about our neighbourhood' and 'Father God, we pray for the not-so-good things about our neighbourhood'.

Among the good things you may have a picture of a local person running in a marathon. This could be accompanied by a prayer written by one of the children:

Dear Lord Jesus, thank you for the people who are doing good things to help others. Thank you for this lady who is running in a marathon to raise money to give to the children's hospital. Thank you for giving her the energy and strength to do this. In Jesus' name. Amen.

Among the not-so-good things, you may have an article on speeding vehicles which could be accompanied by a prayer like this:

Father God, please help drivers to be more careful on the roads and not to drive too fast. Help them to think about children playing. Help them to remember that they are not always in a car and that when they are walking along the road they want to be able to cross safely. Amen.

The findings can be shared with others in the group or in the church by displaying the prayer board or scrapbook for everyone to see. Adults can also be encouraged to pray as they remember their community together before the Lord.

You may have chosen to interview people by using a tape recorder, video or questionnaire. The children can use these to help them to know what to pray about and the video can be shown, or extracts from the tape recording listened to, when sharing with others. To do this it will probably be necessary to edit, so this method is more time-consuming, but older children usually enjoy the challenge!

The children may have their own ideas too. What would they like to see happening in their neighbourhood? What additional facilities would they like to have available? For example, better and safer play areas, a swimming pool or leisure centre, a cinema, better access or transport to local venues. Or maybe they can thank God because they do have access to these facilities.

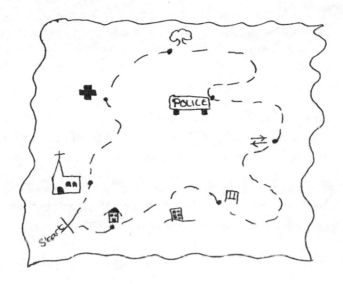

35. Prayerwalk

Prayerwalking is exactly as the name suggests – it's praying as you walk. Children old enough to walk to school with their friends can prayerwalk on their own in small groups. Younger children need to be accompanied. Prayerwalking with an organised group of children, like a Sunday group, will need supervision.

What you need

Others to prayerwalk with

Using the idea

As you walk around your town you can pray for anything that comes to mind. It may be a person you pass in the street, the people behind the doors in the houses, the postman on his bike, the milkman, the bus driver, the passengers on the bus, buildings used by different groups.

If you are walking down residential streets, maybe the children know of people living in these roads whom they can pray for. The prayers may go like this:

Father God, we pray for [Name]. We know how sad she is. She's missing her rabbit. Help her to know that you are with her and that you understand. Amen.

Lord Jesus, please help [Name] to get better quickly. Amen.

If you don't know the needs of the people who live in the road or pass you in the street, suggest that the children ask the Lord to show them how to pray. Otherwise, they could pray a general prayer like:

Father God, bless the people who live in these houses. Amen.

Father God, may something happen today that will help these people to come to know Jesus. Amen.

If the children pray in tongues, this may be a good time for them to pray in their special prayer language. They can be doing this quietly as they walk along. The idea is for them not to draw attention to what they are doing, but to be walking along naturally.

Prayerwalking with your Sunday group needs good

supervision. Make sure that you have consent forms from the children's parents as required by your church's child protection policy. Plan the route and decide where you will stop. Pray together at these places. This can be structured so that the children are encouraged to pray specifically. By stopping at the school, the police station, the library, the doctor's surgery, the town hall, the children have a specific focus for their prayers.

If your stopping place is the school, you can encourage the children to pray for their teachers, for the children in their class, and for any school-related issues that they are aware of, such as bullying. They could do this one after the other, or all of them could pray at the same time. You may even prefer the prayer to be leader-led. For example:

Father God, we pray for this school; for the headteacher and the teachers, those who cook the meals and those who keep the school clean; for the parents who go in to help; and especially for the children. May it be a safe place, a place where they can learn, a place where they can enjoy being with their friends. We claim this school for you, Lord, and we pray for those who know you, teachers and children, that they will have an effect on the school and how it develops. Thank you, Lord. Amen.

We prayed for a school some years ago while out prayer-walking. At that time even the local vicar could not gain access to the school to take assemblies or speak to classes. We claimed the school for the Lord and prayed against any hold on it that was not of God. Within a short time there was a change of headteacher and one of our children's evangelists was able to go in and lead an after school fun time. The school continues to welcome Christian visitors and supports a midweek voluntary Christian group. Prayerwalking works!

If older children want to prayerwalk in a group on their own, then it's best for them to discuss this with you so that you can talk to them about where they are going and make sure that you are happy about their safety. Prayerwalking on their way to school is ideal, but they should bear in mind that being in a hurry because they are late does not mix well with prayerwalking! Younger children can prayerwalk too. They just need someone to take them.

Song

Come, walk with me (*SOFK*)

36. Stained-glass windows

Visit a church in your area that has a stained-glass window.
Stained-glass windows make excellent visual aids. They
usually tell a story. This may be a story from the Bible, but
it may be a local story. Sometimes the picture shows a
famous Christian from the past. Often there is a plaque
underneath which may say who presented the window to
the church. This may have been done in memory of
someone, or in memory of those who died in the World
Wars.

What you need

Suitable stained-glass windows

119

Using the idea

The windows have more than one purpose, so can be used
for prayer in more than one way. One way to pray is to look
at why the window was installed. If it was in memory of
those who died in the World Wars, then we can thank God
for the sacrifice that these young men and women from our
town made on behalf of others. Prayer can develop from
this, maybe praying for peace in the world – in places like
Northern Ireland and the Middle East.

If the window was donated to the church by a church
leader, the Sunday school or a past vicar, the children could
pray about the past, present and future of the church and
its witness in the town. For example:

> *Father God, we thank you that this church has been
> here since the twelfth century and that over the years
> many Christians have gathered together here for
> worship. Thank you for the Christian witness that this
> has been for the town. We pray that this will continue in
> Jesus' name. Amen.*

ADDITIONAL IDEA

What was it like to be there?

The windows can be used to pray for ourselves as we see
ourselves, say, looking up at Jesus on the cross. In our imagination, we might be with the children coming to Jesus, or
among the crowd as Jesus fed the five thousand. Ask the
children to look at an appropriate window, and as they do
so, take them on a walk in their imaginations. For example,
'Imagine that you were there when Jesus was put on the
cross. You watch as the soldiers make Jesus and the other

two men carry their crosses. You see the effort involved in trying to drag them up the hill. A man is pulled out of the crowd and forced to carry the cross for Jesus. You watch them pass by, the dust rising from the ground. Then you hear the nails being hammered into their hands. You are swept along by the crowd and you see the crosses standing together. You read the notice on top of each cross, telling of their crime. On Jesus' cross you read the words: "This is Jesus, the King of the Jews." You hear the Jewish priests making fun of Jesus. You see the soldiers throwing lots for his clothes. Then it is noon, and the whole country becomes dark. It is dark for three hours, then you hear Jesus say, "My God, my God, why have you rejected me?" The next thing you know, Jesus has died. You see the women standing at a distance, and like you they are lost in their own thoughts and sadness.'

Conclude with a prayer. This could be one that you say, or one that they can say with you, either out loud or in their heads. The prayer is a response to where they have been in their imaginations. In this instance it might be:

Lord Jesus, thank you for doing all this for me. Amen.

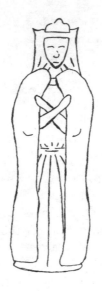

37. Brass rubbing

Exploring our community can take us into the parish church. There are often very interesting things to look at in these churches. Many old churches contain brasses and, with permission, it may be possible to take a brass rubbing. These are usually very effective and can be taken home.

What you need

Brass rubbing wax or thick wax crayons
Cartridge paper
Permission may be needed, and churches sometimes charge a fee

Using the idea

Place the paper over the brass and secure with masking tape. Gently rub over the paper with the wax, and a copy of the brass will appear on the paper. The rubbing can be taken home and used as part of considering our past. Who was this person? Did they influence the growth of Christianity in this town? Maybe the person was a local dignitary. Finding out about the person can lead to praying about the history of the church and its effect upon the town.

You could thank God for the life of this person. Thank God for the influence that this person had. Pray for the work that continues in this church or town as a result of their life. If members of the family are still alive, you could pray for this family.

38. Litter

Try a litter walk, where children can become aware of how people are not caring for your town. For their own protection, advise children not to pick up the litter unless you have gone out with this specific purpose in mind and they are wearing thick gardening gloves. Litter can be contaminated in many ways – by animals, by drug addicts dropping syringes or by other offensive substances or articles. Some of these may be a danger to the children's health.

What you need

Notepad and pencil
Camera

Display board or card and glue
Collage materials (if required)

Using the idea

Jot down thoughts, make a sketch or take photographs. These could be displayed in a group project to heighten awareness of the problem. As part of the project, a litter collage could be made (although not necessarily using litter collected from the streets). Crisp packets, sweet papers, ice lolly wrappers, drinks cans and so on could all be collected with the idea of making a safe display of the kinds of things people drop which become litter.

You could consider with the children how God must feel about the way we treat the town where we live. You could look up Bible references on the responsibility we have to take care of the earth – for example Genesis 1:28; 2:15 – and pray:

Father God, you created the earth and found it to be very good. Help us to look after what you have made and to keep it beautiful for you. Amen.

The children could write down their thoughts and then use these in prayer. Maybe the prayer will include saying 'sorry' to God on behalf of those who leave the town in such a mess. They might also like to think about what they could do to help look after their neighbourhood.

Father God, we are sorry that people are spoiling our town by dropping litter. Help us not to be one of them. Amen.

ADDITIONAL IDEA

Rhymes, songs, raps, poems, psalms

The thoughts, sketches or photographs could develop into writing a rhyme, song, rap, poem or psalm as a prayer. For example:

> Litter in the playground,
> Litter in the street.
> Lord take the litter from under our feet.
>
> Litter in the basket,
> Litter in the bin.
> God made a perfect world for us to live in.

Hannah Dyer

This could be shared with others – either with the rest of the Sunday group or, if appropriate, with the congregation.

39. Books

Looking at books can be an introduction to praying for your town. Books are available on many related topics and can be borrowed from the public library. If you are doing this with children in your family, visiting the library is an adventure in itself.

What you need

Books appropriate for the age of your child or group
For younger children, look in the picture-book section of the library

128   MY NEIGHBOURHOOD

Using the idea

Older children can use the books to find out things for
themselves. You may want to make this into a project. With
younger children, read the book together, with them following by looking at the pictures. Talk about the pictures
and what you are finding out. Pray for your town based on
the topic you have been looking at in the book – for
example, the water supply:

> *Father God, thank you for the people who first laid the
> water supply to our town. We take water so much for
> granted. It is just something that comes out of our taps.
> We forget that it has not always been like this. Help us
> to appreciate it and not waste it. Amen.*

You may be able to arrange to visit the water treatment
works so that the children can see for themselves what
happens to the water.

You may also want to think about and pray for the
people you know who do the jobs in your town that you've
been reading about. Younger children may like to draw pictures.

> *Father God, we pray for [Kerry] as she serves the custom-
> ers in the supermarket (or [Jane] as she stamps the books
> in the library, or [Simon] as he works in the post office,
> or the roadsweeper as he keeps the streets and footpaths
> clean, etc.). Help her to enjoy her work and to keep
> smiling, even when she is tired at the end of the day. May
> her smile encourage her customers. Thank you for her,
> Lord, and for the work she does. In Jesus' name. Amen.*

The children could be encouraged to compare life in their
town with life in towns in other countries.

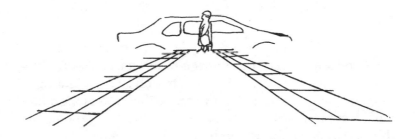

40. Special guests

This idea is more likely to happen in a group situation, although some families may like to choose people to visit their home. Our family has enjoyed finding out about people in this way.

A member of your congregation could be invited to visit your group. They could be a nurse, a children's librarian, a teacher, a milkman, a postman, a bus driver, a shopkeeper ... the possibilities are as great as the number of people willing to come. If the children take to the idea, they may want to interview a number of people on different occasions and build up a broader picture of life in their neighbourhood from real people who are a part of it.

What you need

Willing visitors who are able to relate well to the age of the children in your group or family

Using the idea

Explain to your guest beforehand the aim of their visit and what you would like the children to learn as a result of it. Advise them not to talk for too long, and suggest that they bring lots of things to look at to make their job in the community come alive for the children. Ideally, these should be things that the children can handle or 'have a go' with. For example: a fireman's helmet (the children will enjoy trying it on), a doctor's stethoscope (hearing their own or their friend's heart beat can be fun), or a snake to stroke if your visitor happens to work at a nearby zoo!

Having listened to your guest telling them about their work and handled things they have brought, the children can pray for the work they do in the community. You may want to ask your guest to tell you what they would specifically like prayer for, otherwise the prayer can be more general to their work. Praying for your guest and the work they are doing should be encouraging and upbuilding for them, as well as being a focus of prayer for the children.

The youngest children's prayer may be something like:

Father God, please bless Nurse [Smith] in her work. Amen.

Older children may pray:

Father God, please be with [Alex] as he delivers the post. Help him to be happy and cheerful as he talks to people on their doorsteps. Protect him from the dogs

that bark loudly and would bite his hand if they got the chance. Thank you for the job he does. We all like getting letters. Amen.

If your children and your guest are happy for prayer with the laying on of hands, then the children can lay hands on the guest as they pray for God's blessings for them.

ADDITIONAL IDEA

Interviews

Older children may like to interview the visitor by asking prepared questions and using a notepad and pencil, tape recorder or video to record the answers. Questions could include the following:

- How long have you been a nurse (police officer, milkman, or whatever)?
- What do you enjoy most about your job?
- What do you enjoy least?
- What is the most common injury that you treat (or crime committed in the town, etc.)?

The children can write down their suggestions and decide who asks which question.

If the special guest is not a Christian, it may not be appropriate to pray with them, but the children can use the information gained to pray about their work. Most guests will be pleased to know that the children care enough to pray for them.

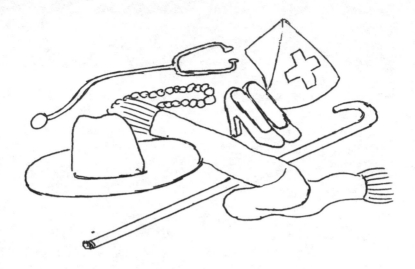

41. Pretend play

This idea is more suited to the younger child who enjoys pretend play. Playing enables the child to imagine what it is like to do a particular job. The ideas of what to play are as creative as the child's imagination. Most young children play shops, doctors and nurses, libraries, schools or post offices. You can take your lead from the children, but if you want to look at a particular job, suggest the game.

What you need

Props for your particular game. For example:

Shops: a till and some things to buy, depending on the type of shop (mini cereal boxes, empty washing-up liquid bottles, bars of soap – whatever you have to hand and are happy for the children to play with).

Libraries: some books, cards to represent the library tickets and a stamp for the books (this could be used on a piece of paper rather than on the books themselves).

Doctors and nurses: a doctor's set would be useful. Nurse's uniforms could be worn.

'Dressing-up' clothes or hats can be chosen with a prayer focus in mind, e.g. the emergency services. Police hats, fireman's hats or the whole uniform could be available for the children to play with.

Using the idea

Enjoy playing, and then pray for the people you've been playing. For example, playing shops enables the child to imagine what it is like to sell as well as to buy. You could ask questions like: What is it like setting up the shop? Did you like buying best or selling? Then pray about what it is like to be the shopkeeper, the check-out operator and the customer.

Another idea is to let the children take it in turns to choose some clothes or a hat and then together they can pray for the work that person does. You may want to talk to the children about the jobs these people do to help them know how to pray. The children's prayers may be like these:

Heavenly Father, thank you for our doctors and nurses. Please help them to know how best to treat people who are ill. Help them to be kind and understanding. In Jesus' name. Amen.

Father God, keep the firemen safe as they fight fires.

Please help people not to start fires on purpose but to take care of other people's property. Amen.

Father God, be with the ambulance men as they drive quickly to get people to hospital. Help them to make the right decisions as they drive fast with their lights flashing. Help them to know the best thing to do for the people they are taking. Thank you, Lord. Amen.

42. Let's go shopping

To help with the shopping can be a young child's delight and an older child's chore.

What you need

A shopping expedition

Using the idea

You could thank God for the food you are buying. You could think about where it is coming from and pray for the farmer, the manufacturer, etc. You could think about the shopworker, the check-out operator, the shelf-stacker.

These become the ideas for prayer.

> *Father God, we thank you for the food we've bought today. Thank you for the people who have been making it for us [you could choose your child's favourite food here, e.g. breakfast cereal], the farmer who grew the grain, the people who made it into breakfast cereal, the person who stacked it on the shelf and the check-out operator where we paid the bill. Thank you that we have such tasty food to enjoy. Amen.*

The prayer should be appropriate for the age of the children. Encourage the children to pray their own prayers.

43. Charities

Various types of fundraising go on within communities, from carnivals to jumble sales. Taking part in these events can be fun. Talking about the charities being helped can lead to prayer.

What you need

A charity event to join in with or one you have planned yourself

Using the idea

One of our older groups regularly planned their own sponsored fun activity to raise money for the Macmillan nurses. This led to praying for the nurses and for the patients they care for.

> *Lord God, please help the Macmillan nurses to be able to care for people dying from cancer. May these last days of their lives be free from pain and treasured times for their families. Amen.*

Fundraising ideas include:

- Sponsored walks.
- Making and selling cakes.
- A coin trail.
- Car washing.

There are some activities that children are not allowed to take part in and others where permission is needed if they involve the general public, so it is better to restrict any fundraising activities to church and people you know if they are not part of a town event.

SECTION 5: MY COUNTRY

If . . . you are careful to obey my commands . . . I will grant peace in the land. (Leviticus 26:3, 6, NIV)

We are citizens of the country into which we are born, and as we grow up we assimilate the culture of our community and are bound by its laws and traditions. We can learn how life used to be and how this affects our lives today, how our country is governed, and how our nation relates to other countries. We represent our country to others when we go abroad. How concerned are we about our country and the decisions taken on our behalf? Children, of course, are not unduly concerned about something unless it affects them directly, so how can we get them praying?

44. Royal Family

I always find it helpful to see pictures of the people I am praying for and to know something about them. This helps motivate me in prayer. The Royal Family, like any other family, need our prayers, but who are they? They seem to have everything, but do they?

What you need

Books, photographs and newspaper articles about the Royal Family (you may need to be selective)

Using the idea

You could choose a member of the Royal Family to find out about. Maybe start with the Queen. What is special about her? She has been crowned by the people to be the head of our country. She has received prayers and anointing for this task by the church. She is head of the Church of England. She is head of the Commonwealth of Nations. She has promised to serve the country as Queen. What does all this mean? What responsibilities go with it? She is also a wife, a mother, a grandmother, an aunt. The children's prayer may go something like this:

> *Father God, thank you for our Queen and for her long service to our country. Be with her in all she has to do. Help her to have time for her family and friends. Give her your courage and strength to do all that she is expected to do as our Queen. In Jesus' name. Amen.*

Finding out about her, her family and her work will help us in our praying; likewise for other members of the Royal Family. If there is anything highlighted in the press, then maybe you could look at this with the children and talk about how to pray. These prayers could be placed in a prayer book or on a prayer board, together with pictures or articles.

ADDITIONAL IDEAS

National anthem

The national anthem is like a prayer for the Queen and also for our nation.

What you need

Copies of the verses of the national anthem. These two seem to be the most appropriate for this idea:

> God save our gracious Queen
> Long live our noble Queen,
> God save the Queen!
> Send her victorious,
> Happy and glorious,
> Long to reign over us,
> God save the Queen!
>
> Thy choicest gifts in store
> On her be pleased to pour,
> Long may she reign;
> May she defend our laws,
> And ever give us cause
> To sing with heart and voice
> God save the Queen!

Using the idea

Look at the words and talk about what they mean, remembering that 'save' carries the meaning of 'preserve, protect and prosper' as well as salvation from sin. You could get the children to rewrite the national anthem in prayer form. Verse 2 could go something like this:

Heavenly Father, please give to our Queen all the gifts that she needs to be the head of our country. As she gets older, may she have enough energy for her work. Help her to defend your laws for our country and to encourage us not to lose what is good. Amen.

Dressing up

Younger children might like to dress up as different members of the Royal Family. You could talk to them about the character they are representing and use this for prayer. For example, the children could pray for the work of the Princess Royal with Save the Children.

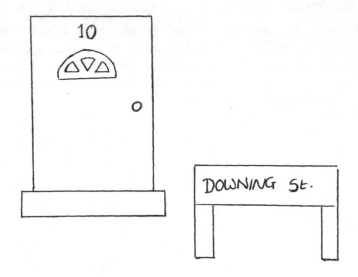

45. The Government

The Government needs wisdom as it seeks to lead our country. Newspapers and the television keep us up to date with developments, and we can use these to help us as we pray. Playing a game as you pray may make this more interesting!

Newspapers and television

What you need

Newspaper articles
Television news

Using the idea

Using the newspaper articles or the television news for ideas of what to pray, the children can pray for the Government and any important decisions it is about to make or international meetings it will be attending. This may be the time for the children to find out the names of the Prime Minister or leader of the Opposition if they don't already know them.

There may be an issue that the Government is addressing that is particularly relevant or of interest to children, and this may be the time to pray for the Government, as the children will more readily identify with the issue. For example:

> *Dear Lord Jesus, please help the Government to make the right decision about our schools and not overload our teachers with lots of extra work. Amen.*

A game

One way of using this in a game is to list the issues for prayer on a sheet of paper or on an acetate to give the children ideas of what they can pray for. There is a fun element in all of this, so enjoy playing various games, then choose one game – for example, passing a ball randomly round the group.

What you need

A ball
A sheet of paper or acetate for OHP and marker pens

Using the idea

As each child has their turn at catching the ball, they choose one of the prayer issues for their prayer. The ball can be passed to the next person by throwing, kicking, dribbling or sending it backwards through the child's legs. The game can be fast-moving with short prayers. For example:

Lord Jesus, we pray for the Prime Minister. Help him to lead the Government wisely. Amen.

Lord Jesus, be with the Foreign Secretary as he meets for talks tomorrow. Amen.

Games like this can, of course, be used with any prayer topic.

46. Commemorative stamps

Have a look at the latest commemorative stamps. From
these you can find out what is thought to have been important for our country. This may have been a national sport-
ing event, a scientific discovery, a royal wedding, a
contribution to the arts. Looking at the stamps can give us
ideas for prayer.

What you need

Commemorative stamps

Using the idea

Look at the stamps, talk about the event, person or discovery and why this is being remembered, and let this conversation move into prayer. For example:

We thank you, Father, for the RSPCA and the care they give to abandoned animals. Help people in this country to take proper care of their animals. Amen.

Lord Jesus, I like reading books. Thank you for the people who write them. Amen.

ADDITIONAL IDEAS

International concerns

Stamps can also lead us into praying for international relationships and concerns.

What you need

Foreign stamps
An atlas or world map

Using the idea

You may want to find the stamp of a particular country to focus on for prayer, or you may be happy for the children each to pick a stamp from any country. You could find the country in an atlas or on a world map. In addition to the map, children's atlases often have information about the country which is helpful for a quick overview. If you know of any difficulty that we as a nation have with this particular country, use the stamp to focus prayer on this problem.

Collecting stamps

Many children enjoy stamp collecting as a hobby. Some children may like to collect stamps for their own prayer book. Children can also be encouraged to collect stamps to send to a missionary group for fundraising. They may like to include the whole church in this by making and placing a stamp collection box in church. We have done this, and many in the church have been pleased because they had wanted to be able to pass their stamps on to someone. Handling and sorting the stamps can lead to praying.

47. Living museums

Museums of buildings, industry or history usually appeal to children, especially if they are hands-on or 'living' museums. These show life in the past, often with atmosphere and 'voice-overs' creating a sense of really being there. There may be experiments to take part in, as in a chemical museum we visited, or trams to ride on and coal mines to go into, as in the case of a museum reflecting daily life in homes, shops, coal mines and other local industry in earlier days.

What you need

A visit to a living museum

Using the idea

Let visiting the museum stimulate prayer and go with the children's ideas. You might be able to pray while you are there (in a similar way to prayerwalking), or you could pray when you are at home or back in your group. First and foremost, the children will be focused on the visit and wanting to enjoy it for its own sake. Talking informally with the children will help them to bring their experiences into prayer. Some ideas might be:

- Thank God for people who brought about changes in living conditions.
- Thank God for people who brought about changes in attitudes towards things like the slave trade.
- Pray for people whose health has been affected by the jobs they did when they were younger.
- Pray about safety in industry today.

ADDITIONAL IDEA

Historic buildings

Castles, cathedrals, stately homes and listed buildings are all part of our heritage. These too can be visited and used to stimulate prayer. The children can thank God for the skills to build, for the beauty of these places, for the peace, for the coolness they provide on a hot day. Again, many of these buildings have guides, voice-overs or other helps to make the visit as interesting as possible, and this information can provide ideas for prayer.

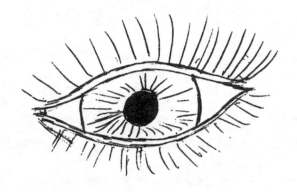

48. I-Spy

What do children do during long car journeys? You may take activities for them to do, but otherwise they look out of the window or listen to tapes. An idea for families is to look out of the window and pray about what they see.

What you need

A journey by car

Using the idea

As the children look out of the window you could ask: What can you see? This can be played as a game. For example: 'What do you see?' They may reply: 'I see a school.' Then pray for the children who go to this school:

Father God, please be with the children who go to this school. Help them to want to learn, to listen to their teachers, to enjoy being with their friends and to care for one another. Amen.

Or they might say: 'I see a church.' Then you could pray for the children in their Sunday groups and clubs; for the church, that it will be a place where people who live nearby will feel welcome; for people who will get married in the church; for God's blessings upon the church and its leaders.

This idea can be used with whatever the children see. It might be a man walking his dog, a flock of sheep, a corn-field, an electricity pylon. The choice is theirs!

49. Not the six o'clock news

No, but it could be a children's TV news programme like *Newsround*! Watching the news does make us aware of what is going on, both in our country and globally, and this can give us up-to-the-minute information for prayer. This idea is possibly easier with your own children, as you can sit down together to watch *Newsround*, but it is possible to challenge children in a prayer group, and even in a Sunday group, especially if there is something major happening. In a group, you may want to set up a game for the prayer time.

Television

What you need

Watch *Newsround* or a similar programme
Pencil and paper

Using the idea

If using this idea within a family, encourage the children to
jot prayer ideas down on a piece of paper as they watch.
Use these for prayer either after *Newsround* or, more
likely, later on. Children in prayer groups can be asked to
do the same, but they could write their prayers into their
prayer books (see Idea 55) to share with the prayer group
when they meet. Children in Sunday groups may not be
quite so committed to prayer. However, if there is a major
disaster, you could suggest that they keep up to date with
what is happening by watching *Newsround* and then pray
for the people involved. When the group is together on
Sunday, you could talk about what has been happening
during the week and this may lead into prayer as a group.

By watching a programme like *Newsround*, children can
be encouraged to think about wider issues rather than just
those that affect them directly. If they are regular viewers,
they may be motivated to pray about many issues as they
are raised. For example, conservation, pollution, homeless-
ness, the elderly, day care for young children, care of
animals, protection of endangered species, government
decision-making on schools, new motorways and the effect
on the environment, our country's relationship with
Europe or the rest of the world.

A group game

For the more active, set up a game for the prayer time. One example is skittles.

What you need

Version 1: skittles or plastic bottles, a ball, paper, pens, sticky tape
Version 2: skittles or plastic bottles, a ball, card, pens

Using the idea

1. Write out the prayer ideas and attach them to skittles or plastic bottles. Place the skittles in a line for the children to knock down. The children choose a skittle to aim for and roll the ball towards it. As it falls they pick it up and pray for the issue attached to the skittle. The next child has their turn.

2. The prayer issues could be written on cards and numbered 0 to 6 and the skittles arranged in a triangular formation. The children take it in turns to knock down the skittles. However many skittles they knock down they take the card of the same number and use this for the subject of their prayer. They pray their prayer before the next child has their turn. You will need several prayers for each number.

50. Peace in our land

All of us want to live in peace. We want to be able to raise our families in security and to be able to go about our daily lives without fear. To this end, each country has its own security forces. These include the police for internal matters and the armed forces for our national defence.

What you need

Aluminium foil

Using the idea

Give each child a piece of foil about 15cm × 15cm and ask

them to make it into a sword or a gun. Ask them to hold the sword or gun and pray for the armed forces as they defend our country or act as peace-keeping forces in other countries.

> *Father God, we pray for the soldiers in Bosnia. Protect them and help them as they protect others. Amen.*

Then ask the children to make the sword or gun into something else. (If they are not sure what, you could suggest a plate or a bowl, or even a ploughing blade!) The children then hold this and pray for peace between their own and other countries. Use this time to pray for countries that are in conflict, or for incidences of unrest or violence within our own country. This can also include prayer for the police force and those who uphold law and order in the land.

> *Lord God, we pray for peace where there is fighting. We pray for those who are caught up in the fighting, especially children. We ask you to show the men who fight that there are other ways of working things out without hurting people so much. Amen.*

Songs

Peace I give to you (*JP*)
Peace is flowing like a river (*SOFK*)

51. Church leaders

Church leaders hold positions of leadership nationally as well as locally. They are in positions to influence attitudes and decisions and, to do this, they need to be in places where their voices will be heard. This may be in the House of Lords for the bishops or at community meetings for local church leaders such as vicars and ministers.

Their main role is to preach the word of God and to care for their church members (and in churches like the Church of England this also extends to the whole of their parish). They have a lot to do, both in the church and in the community, and need our prayers. What can we pray?

Interview

What you need

Notebook and pencil or cassette recorder
Card (optional)

Using the idea

The children could ask their church leader what he or she would like them to pray for. To help them to remember they could make notes or use a cassette recorder. The children can take these prayer requests away with them to pray about during the week. If there are a lot, each child could take one thing. You could give them a piece of card to write this down.

If the children would like to pray regularly for their church leader, after the initial interview the church leader may prefer to give the children subsequent prayer requests in writing.

Symbols of office

If the leaders of your church wear, or have, any symbols of office you could ask them to show these to the children. For example, bishops in the Church of England wear a special hat (called a mitre) as a symbol of office. This shows that they are appointed to lead the church. They carry a staff (a crosier), which is a bit like a shepherd's crook, to show that they look after people, and they wear a big cross to show that they represent Jesus. Unless the bishop is already coming to your church, he may not be able to show these to the children, in which case you may have to look at pictures of these things. If he is coming, though, do ask him – preferably in advance!

Alternatively, the symbol may be a Bible. Perhaps your church leader would show the children the Bible he or she was presented with when ordained or appointed.

What you need

Symbol or picture of symbol

Using the idea

Use these symbols to pray. For example:

Thank you, Lord, that the bishop's staff reminds us that he leads his people, like the shepherds in Bible times, walking in front of the flock. The shepherd would use his crook to help a sheep out of danger. The shepherd watched out for his sheep. He found them good pasture and protected them from wild animals. Please help the bishop as he cares for people. Amen.

Dear Lord, we know that the Bible is your word. Please help our minister to have time to study it so that he can teach us more about Jesus. Amen.

Section 6: The World

First, I tell you to pray for all people, asking God for what they
need and being thankful to him. (1 Timothy 2:1)

Getting into the lives of other people is not easy, especially
when those people live in other countries. We need as many
stimuli as we can find to help us – however old we are!
Newspapers and television can keep us up to date with the
current news, and older children can read and watch these
themselves. Younger children need the information shared
in a way they can understand.

One of my greatest delights has been our children's
prayer group which we called Stopwatch Club because we
were affiliated to Stopwatch – part of Chime Worldwide, a
resource for children, their parents and leaders who want
to pray for the nations. We also used material from
Tearfund and Toybox Charity. These, and other groups,
produce project packs which are excellent for getting to
know about a country, and we have found them an invaluable help to our prayers. Addresses for these groups can be
found in Part Three.

The world of young children is very much that with
which they are familiar. It is hard for them to understand
what life is like for someone else, but that does not mean
that they are not interested. For some years now we have

been talking to children of three and four years old at the Soul Survivor and New Wine/Lakeside conferences about street children in Guatemala. We have used a puppet to tell the children about life on the streets. This has been our introduction to prayer (see Idea 53) and the children have wanted to know more.

52. Candles

Candles symbolise the light of Christ and in this prayer idea they represent the light of Christ being taken to the nations.

What you need

A nightlight candle in a jar for each child
Matches and taper (optional)
Map of the world

Using the idea

Look at the world map with the children and ask each child

to choose a country. Let the children tell you of any prayer need that they are aware of for that country then, as each child takes their turn to pray, light their candle. The children place their candles on the country for which they are praying.

53. Puppets

With young children you don't have to be a puppeteer or have sophisticated puppets to capture their interest. You just need the courage to have a go! With older children, you may want to practise a few times in front of a mirror!

For some years now we have used a simple glove puppet at Soul Survivor and New Wine. Named Perro (the Spanish word for dog), he is a Dalmatian and, because he is telling the children about the street children in Guatemala, he lives in a cardboard box. Perro is a street dog and in true Sooty style he whispers into my ear as he tells us all about life on the streets. Such is the imagination of the children that many think he is a real dog until they touch him. Others are not so easily fooled!

Older children love puppets too. Our experience in church and school is that the puppets need to get bigger as the children get older! Muppet-style puppets are very popular with older children and they also like to work these for themselves. (See Part Three for address of puppet suppliers.)

What you need

A suitable puppet

Using the idea

The puppet is used to capture the interest of the children and provides the focus for the teaching. Taking the idea of street children, the dog puppet we used spoke into my ear from a cardboard box on my arm. Each day at the conference he talked to us about something different. We covered topics like what the children had to eat, how they found their food, the problems of keeping warm, where they went to sleep, what happened if they didn't feel very well, the people who might help them, as well as the dangers of living on the streets.

The children looked forward to seeing Perro and this led us into praying about the street children and the problems they face.

ADDITIONAL IDEAS

Developing the idea further

This could be part of a whole session or series of sessions on street children. The overall theme might be 'Jesus cares – we care', and activities appropriate to the age of the children can be included. If the session's topic is 'What do the children have to eat?' you could make sandwiches or decorate biscuits. The children could colour in different foods and display these or draw their favourite meal on a paper plate. The children could write their prayers and display them on a prayer board. These ideas are explained later in this section. How you use the idea for prayer and link it with other ideas depends on how much time you have and how many children you are dealing with.

Making puppets

Making puppets for the children to use or to remind them to pray works well. We made mini Perros by photocopying enough pictures of Perro (see picture above), cutting them out and giving one to each child. They coloured it in and then stuck it onto a paper cone that we had made by cutting out a two inch square piece of paper, folding it in half and wrapping it round the child's finger with the point at the top, sticking it together with sticky tape and attaching the picture to the pointed end, again with sticky tape. This can be folded over on itself so that it is not visible.

The teaching can be given using finger puppets. You could make the finger puppets together and then each child can wear their finger puppet as you tell them what you want them to know. This can be adapted for any topic you may wish to cover. If you want the children to think about where bananas come from, and the people who live in that country, you could make banana finger puppets!

54. This is their life

If your church has link missionaries they may be able to send photographs of themselves and the work they are doing. These will help the children to see what life is like for someone else in another place. Missionary societies can be contacted for resources. I have been amazed at the interest that even the youngest children have in looking at pictures and photographs.

What you need

Suitable photographs or pictures (when talking to a large number of children, it helps if these are big)

Using the idea

Use the photographs or pictures to talk about the people in the pictures. If you can, tell the children the names of the people they are looking at. It also helps if you can tell the children their story. This brings the photographs to life. These are real people, real children, real grown-ups, and this is what is happening in their lives. This will stimulate prayer.

Father God, [Seth] is hungry. Please bring rain to his country so that the crops will grow and the people will have enough food. Thank you, Lord. Amen.

ADDITIONAL IDEAS

Collecting money

Seeing the pictures and praying may also motivate action. The children may want to help, as our children in Stopwatch Club did. They added their giving money to the church's donation to send to Tanzania at a time when that country was facing famine. The money was being given to help the church there provide food for those who needed it until the next crop could be grown by the farmers.

Making a collage

The children can cut pictures out of magazines and stick them onto a piece of paper to make a collage. Together you could talk about the pictures and then pray about the things you have discussed.

Lord, thank you for the happy smiling faces of these children. Thank you that the rains have come and that they can play in the puddles. Amen.

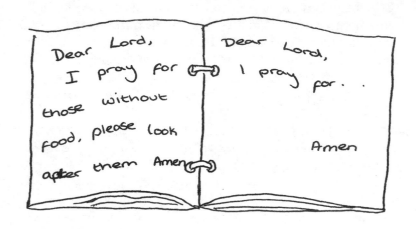

55. Making your own prayer book

We have found that making a prayer book is a good way to record prayers for children in other countries and answers to prayers. In a prayer group setting, the children have prayers that they can share. At home they have their own prayer resource.

What you need

Six sheets of A4 white or coloured paper for each child
Hole-punch
Wool to tie
Felt-pens or crayons to decorate

Using the idea

Fold the sheets of paper together to make a book and punch two holes near the folded edge. Thread the wool through and tie. The children can decorate the cover as they wish, maybe writing on it 'My prayer book' or 'Praying for the nations'. You can decide this together.

As you pray for children in other parts of the world, the children can write their prayers in their prayer book. This may follow a time when you have been looking at pictures or finding out about a particular group of children. They then have some information on which to base their prayers.

If you pray regularly for one group of children and you receive prayer news from the project, you can use this for prayer. The children can also check back in their prayer books when fresh prayer news arrives and see how the Lord has been answering their prayers. Younger children can have their own prayer book too. Their prayers can be drawn.

Writing or drawing prayers can encourage children to speak out their prayers because being able to read them gives them confidence. We found this an invaluable help when our children's prayer group first began.

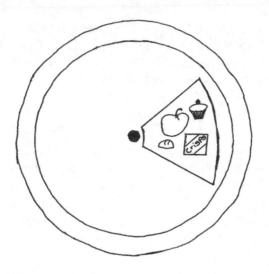

56. Prayer wheel

Making a prayer wheel is a fun way of recording prayer topics. Topics could be a country (e.g. India, Latvia, Guatemala), with pictures of children, families, workers, crops, water, homes, hospitals, schools; or a theme like 'Clean water', with pictures of different clean-water projects around the world.

Other themes might be:

Street children

For this you may want to take one particular country and look at issues like food, keeping warm, health, playing games, dangers and the people who are trying to work with them and help them, or you may want to think about this issue worldwide and so have pictures of children from different countries.

Fair wages

For this you may want to use different products like coffee, tea, cocoa, bananas or tee-shirts, and pray that those who grow and pick the crops or make the tee-shirts will get their fair share of the price we pay for the goods.

Tearfund and Christian Aid produce useful resources for topics. (See Part Three for addresses.)

What you need

Two circles of card: one 100cm radius, one 80cm radius
Pencil, ruler, scissors, glue stick
Felt-pens or crayons
Split pins
Pictures of children, people, countries

Using the idea

Take the larger card and divide it into eight equal sections across the diameter (like the spokes of a wheel). Choose pictures cut into triangular shapes and stick them into the different sections. Divide the smaller card into eight equal sections. Cut one section out of this card and attach it over the top of the larger card using the split pin. Moving the smaller card reveals the prayer topic.

Sections can be named with the prayer topic by writing this in the space on the larger card which can be seen outside the smaller wheel. The smaller wheel can be decorated or entitled 'My prayer wheel'.

The prayer wheel is ready to use. The children turn the smaller circle and the picture that appears in the open section becomes the prayer focus. They use this focus to help them to pray. They can do this in their group if you are all using prayer wheels, or by taking the wheel home and praying in their own prayer times. Prayers might go something like this:

Lord Jesus, I want to pray for the little boy in this picture. He looks hungry and sad, and there are flies on his face. I want to pray that someone will help him by giving him food and loving him. Thank you, Jesus. Amen.

57. Missionary on furlough

Talking to a missionary, an ex-missionary or someone who has been to a foreign country can bring to life the people and their needs. Showing the children photographs, slides or even a short video can help them to identify with the people. Dressing up in the national costume can be fun and so too can eating local food.

What you need

A missionary on furlough
If required: food, a pass-the-parcel, taped music, national dress, pictures, a world map, objects from the country

Using the idea

1. Prepare for the visit

Talk to the missionary and to the children beforehand as part of your, and their, preparation. Maybe the children have questions they would like to ask. These could be written on pieces of paper and placed in a bowl or inter-leaved in a pass-the-parcel. The questions could then be asked as part of a game (see Idea 11). The missionary could also be allowed to ask questions of the children if some of the pieces of paper suggest this.

2. Look on a map

Look up on a map the country where the missionary has been working. The missionary will be happy to talk about the country and they may have objects from the country that the children can pass round. They may also have stamps or a flag that the children can look at. Children seem to enjoy colouring in pictures of flags.

3. Enjoy the day ... food

On the day of the visit, taped music from the country could be played to set the scene and the children could arrive early to prepare the food. The missionary may be able to give you some ideas for this, otherwise many cookbooks do give the country of origin with their recipes. At its simplest, different fruits can be prepared. Many supermarkets label their fruit with the country of origin and if this is the part of the world where your missionary is working, the children may enjoy tasting these fruits. Rather than food from their specific country, you may want to choose the theme of 'food from around the world' for the food part of your gathering, in the context of serving God in all countries.

4. Learn a new greeting, song or dance

Maybe the missionary can teach the children some simple words of greeting or even a song. One missionary we had visit us from Tanzania taught the children a song which they then sang in church. The same could be done with a national dance. The children may like to dress up in national costume. Taking photographs of the children doing this helps them to recall it later and encourages continued prayer.

5. Pray

The purpose of these activities is to see, hear and feel what it is like to live in the country where the missionary is working. This helps us as we pray. We can pray for the way of life in this country – for example, for the children as they collect water each day, as they look for wood to make a fire, as they help their mothers in the fields or their fathers by looking after the goats on the hills. What about going to school or lying in hospital needing medicines that the doctor does not have? Maybe your missionary works with children who don't have a home and have to live on the streets. Hearing about children in other countries from people who work with them helps to personalise the situation.

We can pray for this missionary who is real with his or her own needs. It can be lonely being a missionary. We prayed for our missionary that she would meet someone who would be a friend. We were delighted when we heard that our prayers had been answered.

The children can pray with the missionary. If they are happy to pray out loud, the children can pray for the needs that the missionary has shared with them. If they are used to praying with the laying on of hands (see Idea 3), they can ask the missionary if he or she would be happy for them to pray in this way. We all need prayer.

6. Keep in touch

After the missionary's visit, keep in touch by letter or E-mail. This will encourage the missionary and help the children to be a part of God's work by praying for someone else. The children could visit websites on the Internet to find out more about what is happening in the missionary's country. They may want to extend this to finding out about other countries too and include this information in their prayers. (See Part Three for some website addresses.)

Songs

Go, Go, Go (*SOFK*)
Go, tell it on the mountain (*JP*)

58. Going on a journey

Metaphorically speaking! This can be done in various ways, but the way I favour is to play music from the country in the background, have children close their eyes and encourage them to use their imagination as you tell them a story of life in that country.

What you need

Music from the country
Content for the story from newspapers, television reports, missionary prayerletters, organisations like Tearfund and Toybox Charity or from a book like *50 Five-Minute Stories* by Lynda Neilands (Kingsway Publications), *You Can*

Change the World by Jill Johnstone (OM Publishing) or
You Can Change the World Too by Daphne Spraggett with
Jill Johnstone (OM Publishing)

Using the idea

Your journey takes you to your chosen country. Imagine
the place: an African hut; the Toybox Charity bus on the
streets of Guatemala; sinking a well in India; the atmosphere; the heat or the cold; the rain or lack of it; hungry
tummies; someone bathing your feet, handing out clothes
or shoes; receiving a pair of glasses from England; the story
of street children being offered a home or a job; finding
someone who cares and seeing the love of God in this.

Your prayers will follow the main teaching of the story.
You may be praying for the street children or the people
who help them; for missionary doctors and nurses or for
their patients; for money to sink another well or for the
families that will be able to drink clean water. The prayer
need of your missionary might be for protection against the
people who want them to stop doing their work, or it might
be for the drought in their country to end.

Choose the length of the story to fit the age and attention span of the children. Even young children can be
happy listening to a story in this way if it is not too long. Ask
what you should pray about. Keep this time short. After
they've answered, it may be better to say that those were
the prayers if the children are becoming unsettled.
Alternatively, they could draw or act their prayers.

59. Cardboard city

Pretending is a good way for younger children to get into the lives of children living in other countries. Doing may have more appeal for older children. Younger children could pretend they are living on the streets and have to make a bed out of cardboard boxes and old bits of newspaper. Older children can actually do this with supervision, although the shelter may be a bit more than a cardboard box. Plastic sheeting could be used to create a makeshift tent, and maybe sleeping bags should be allowed if the children are going to sleep out over night, as even in the summer months it can be cold in this country. Obviously you'll want to do this in a safe environment with adequate supervision – perhaps in a garden. Role play brings situations to life and gives us something to recall when praying on other occasions too.

Younger children – pretending

What you need

Cardboard boxes
Newspaper or leaves in autumn (check that they are clean!)

Using the idea

A cardboard box, newspaper or leaves can make a home and a bed for a street child. Use this to talk about street children. Information and project material can be obtained from organisations like Tearfund, Stopwatch and Toybox Charity working with street children in Guatemala (addresses in Part Three). Why are these children on the streets? Where will their food come from? Can they sleep? Will they be warm enough? Who is helping them? Younger children can enjoy role playing as they think about children having no other home. This can naturally lead into praying for these children, or thanking God for their own warm beds. For example:

> I'm really glad I have a bed to sleep in, Jesus. Thank you. Amen.

Older children – doing

What you need

Materials for the shelter (like newspapers, leaves, cardboard boxes, polythene sheeting, etc.)

If you are planning for the children to sleep in it:
Sleeping bags
Food and drinks
Venue, insurance cover, parental consent

Tearfund have an information sheet called *Building Your Own Shanty*, with accompanying discussion questions which you may find helpful.

Using the idea

Older children will be excited at the prospect of making a shelter, especially if they can sleep in it. Whether you feel able to allow them to sleep over will depend on your circumstances, the needs of the children and the availability of adults to supervise the activity. Making the shelter is a useful exercise in itself, enabling the children to empathise with people living in shanty towns, and this can stimulate their prayers. Provide the children with suitable materials, or have them bring some of these with them, and let them have a go at making their shelter. Discuss this with them as they build. Will it stay standing? At the end, talk about the different designs and consider how the children felt about making their shelters. Was it as easy as they first thought? How easy would it be to find the materials they were using if they were living on the streets? What did they think about the time they needed to spend making it? What would it be like to sleep all night outside in a shelter like this? How would they cook their food? What would they do about drinks, washing, going to the toilet? Let this discussion time lead on to prayer.

If sleeping in the shelter

Should you want the children to sleep in the shelter, you will need to give consideration to security, safety and warmth. The children will have to have sleeping bags and the shelter will need to protect them from the weather if you choose to do this activity outside. The alternative is to make the shelter indoors and this solves any problem of keeping away passing members of the general public. If you are outside, choose a closed site. It might be a good idea to have adult leaders stay awake through the night to supervise the activity and an indoor retreat should this become necessary. You may also want to consider your group's insurance cover and maybe take out additional insurance for this event. Your insurance company or denominational youth officer will be able to advise.

You will need parental consent, and parents need to understand that the objective is for the children to feel a certain vulnerability. They are placing themselves in the shoes of street children who have no adults to care for them. However, in reality this is an experience which is being supervised.

If you choose to make your shelter indoors, you could add to the effect by bringing in litter bins and creating your own 'tip' of newspapers, cardboard boxes, sheeting and so on in the corner. To further aid the sense of disorientation and vulnerability, you could play tape recordings of police sirens, crying, dogs barking, etc.

Taking into account the age and needs of the children, draw up a plan for the event. List those things that you consider to be important for the well being of the children, while maintaining a focus on the objective. Plan to use the debrief the next morning for prayer; a prayer breakfast could follow as a celebration for the children's own survival through the night! You could ask questions like: What did it feel like to sleep in your shelter? What sounds did you hear? Were you happy with these sounds? What were you thinking? Did you feel safe? How do you think children feel when they first find themselves living on the streets?

What might it be like after a few months? What would they do for food and clothes?

Follow this with prayer.

Lord Jesus, I'm so glad that I don't have to live on the streets. There is so much I would miss: my parents, my toys, television, the computer, having my meals given to me, clean clothes, a toilet. Be with the children who have nowhere else to live. Be with families living in cardboard cities. Help them to find enough food to eat. Send people to help them. Amen.

60. Make a hut

Craft activities can lead into prayer. This idea uses an African hut, but the craft idea can be used for other countries and other living conditions. If praying for the boat people, you may want to make boats!

Not everyone in Africa lives in a hut. The country is large and many of the people live in towns and in houses, but in the more remote parts the people live in huts. This activity might also look at the animals that live in the country. Do lions or zebras live near the villages? How do the people have a bath? What kind of jobs do the people have? Do the children go to school? Do they wear uniforms? Answers to these questions can be found in project packs obtainable from missionary organisations or in books on individual countries sometimes available from the public library.

What you need

For an African hut:
Strip of paper approximately 8cm × 30cm
Circle of paper with an 8cm radius
Brown or orange crayons
Straw (or art straws or paper drinking straws) and glue for roof (optional)
Sticky tape
Sand and tray for display

Using the idea

1. Make the hut

Colour the strip of paper for the sides of the hut and a circle for the roof with the brown or orange crayons. Cut halfway across the circle and overlap the cut ends to form a cone shape. Stick down with sticky tape. If required, cover with straw or use art straws or paper drinking straws (if these can be found). Take the strip of paper and overlap the shorter ends to form a circle to make the walls of the hut. Check that the cone-shaped roof is going to fit on top of it and, using the sticky tape, stick the ends together. Balance the cone shape on top to make the roof and there you have your hut. The huts can be displayed on sand with other huts to form a village.

2. Find out about the people

Other resources will help you to find out more about the country and the people for whom you want to pray. For the idea above we used a project pack from Tearfund (address in Part Three). There was also an accompanying video which was excellent for helping children appreciate that making a cup of tea is not as easy as they thought when the tea has to be picked, the water collected from the water source, the wood for the fire to heat the water found and, finally, when the water is boiling and the tea is made, the goat has to be milked if you take milk with your tea! This in itself is fuel for prayer and our children's prayer group really enjoyed watching the video.

3. Pray

Prayers followed. For example:

> *Dear Lord, I pray for the people in Tanzania. It must be very hard living there with water so far away. We pray for them as they go to get their water and as they grow their crops and care for their animals. Amen.*

Note: Project packs do change from year to year so you may want to write to Tearfund for information on their latest pack and take that as your prayer focus, using the craft activities suggested to lead the children into prayer.

61. I'm hungry

How often do we hear that? Most children want to eat and love anything which involves food! The idea here is for children to make something they will enjoy eating. You could make sandwiches with younger children, but older children may want to be more adventurous. Bearing in mind the time available and the cost of the ingredients, the choice could be theirs ... or yours! As the food is being made, the idea is to help the children to think about what it might be like to be really hungry.

Sandwiches

What you need

A slice of bread for each child
Blunt knife
Margarine
Fillings such as yeast extract, jam, grated cheese and ham
(*Tip*: If doing this with a group of children, you need to check for food allergies. For example, some children are intolerant of gluten and therefore cannot be given bread, but parents can advise on alternatives. Peanuts and eggs are best avoided)
Greaseproof paper to use as a work mat and then to wrap the sandwiches in if not being eaten immediately
Hand-washing facilities, plus soap and towel

Using the idea

While making the sandwiches you could talk to the children about what they are doing and which fillings they are going to choose. This could lead on to talking about their favourite food and, when the sandwiches are made, thanking God for all the different food that we can enjoy. You may also want the children to think about times when they are hungry. How do they feel? What would it be like if they knew that there wasn't any food in the cupboard? This is how it is for some children. Maybe the rains didn't come so the crops didn't grow, or perhaps there is a war in the country. Children in this country might be hungry too. This can lead on to praying for children who are hungry:

> *Lord Jesus, it's horrible being hungry, but we know that we can soon have food. Be with those who know they can't – with mothers trying to find enough food for their*

*children; with fathers trying to grow crops in poor soil;
with children hunting for food around the rubbish tips.
Help us to care enough to do something to help them.
Amen.*

*Lord God, please help the aid agencies to get food
through to the children in the refugee camps. Protect
them from the fighting. We pray for peace. Amen.*

*Please bring rain. The crops are in the ground and they
need rain to make them grow. Thank you, Lord. Amen.*

Maybe the children want to say 'sorry' for the food they
waste or for the food the richer nations are stockpiling.
Their prayer for this might be:

*We are sorry that we waste food and that we hoard it.
Please, Lord, help our country to share. Amen.*

Making bread

If you have time, you may want to make bread or rolls with
the children.

What you need

A packet of bread or pizza base mix, baking tray, oven

Using the idea

Packets of bread mix or pizza base mix are readily available
in supermarkets and are easily made. If using with a group,
you may want to make the dough up first and let it rise, then
give each child a small piece to make into a roll and add
their identification mark (their initial or own design). Place
each roll on a baking tray and put into the oven as directed.
The bread smells and tastes really good.

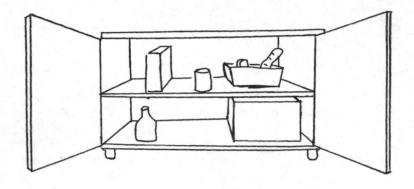

62. What's in the cupboard?

Most of us have tins and packets in our cupboards and many of us read the labels on them to check the contents and their suitability for our children. Labels can also provide ideas for prayer. One idea is to look on the label for the country of origin.

What you need

Tins and packets from the cupboard
Atlas or world map, flag-style labels, mapping pins (optional)

Using the idea

Tins

On a wet day, you could allow the children to get the tins out of your cupboard and to stand them on the table. The country of origin is usually marked on the label, so you could look for this together. Then if, for example, you found some peaches from Greece you could pray:

> *Dear Lord, thank you for the sunlight, the rain and the soil that made the peaches grow. Thank you that you have made them for us to enjoy. We pray for the farmers who care for the peach trees, for the people who pick and pack the fruit and for the supermarkets that sell it to us. May each one have their fair share of the money that we pay for the fruit. Help none of them to be greedy for money. For this fruit is yours for all of us to benefit from. Amen.*

If the children help with the cooking, they could check the country of origin each time they use something from a tin, and together you could pray for that country, or it may be the contents that inspire prayer! For example, dolphin-friendly tuna can turn their prayers to dolphins:

> *Thank you, Lord, that these fishermen are trying not to harm the dolphins when they are catching tuna. Please help all countries to care about what their fishermen are doing. Amen.*

World map

A world map on the kitchen wall could be useful if you use this idea a lot. This will help the children know where the countries are. Flag-style labels bearing the name of the produce could be pinned to the map.

Labels

Using this idea with a group, you could ask the children to bring in labels from tins used at home and together make a scrapbook or poster, adding the children's prayers. An atlas might be helpful for seeing where the country is in the world and finding out something about it. This can give ideas for prayer, as can listening out for anything on the news about that country.

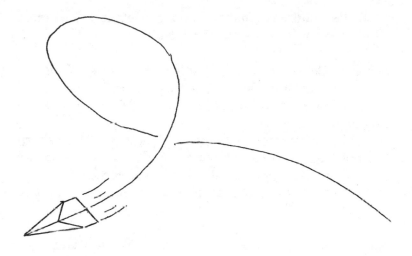

63. Fly a prayer

To get to far away places, we often travel by aeroplane. We can make our prayers travel by aeroplane too by making a paper aeroplane and writing or drawing our prayers onto it! Any prayer can be written on the prayer plane and flown, but having associated aeroplanes with travelling to far away places, praying for children in other countries, mission partners, news items and other concerns would be particularly appropriate.

What you need

A4 sheet of paper, pencil

Using the idea

1. Ask the children to make a paper aeroplane. I think most children would know what to do, but if not:

(a) Take the A4 piece of paper, and fold in half along the vertical. Flatten out.
(b) Fold two top corners to the centre fold to make a triangle.
(c) Fold each corner again into a triangle to make a sharp point at the top of the paper.
(d) Fold in half along the already folded vertical line.
(e) Fold out the wings to form a body. The plane is ready to fly!

Younger children may need you to make the plane for them.

2. Hold the wings and pull apart. Lie the aeroplane on the table and invite the children to write or draw their prayer for 'far away places' on the aeroplane. Re-form the plane.

3. When everyone is ready, fly the planes. Everyone could do this at the same time and, in itself, this could be the prayer. You could then have everyone pick up a plane, read out the prayer and then fly the prayer planes again. Although it may sound noisy and appear chaotic to pray lots of different prayers out loud at the same time, there is power in the spiritual realm when we do so and God hears each one. Children who may feel shy or embarrassed about speaking out their prayer can be released from these feelings as they are caught up in the enjoyment of the activity.

SECTION 7: MYSELF

Remember the Lord in everything you do, and he will show you the right way. (Proverbs 3:6)

We are the ones who know most about ourselves. Or are we? Life can revolve around ourselves whatever age we are, and yet our identity is in Christ. We need to develop that right relationship with God which will enable us to find our true selves and to live a life that pleases him. Jesus modelled that life for us. Jesus taught us by his life that we need to spend time with our Father in heaven. We need to share with God our hopes and fears. We need to receive from God his direction and his peace.

64. I'm special

God has made each of us to be ourselves. We are 'fearfully and wonderfully made' (Psalm 139:14, NIV). This idea is to help children appreciate their uniqueness and the fact that they are special to God.

What you need

Paint or a washable ink pad
Paper

Using the idea

Get the children to place an index finger in the paint or ink and then press it onto the paper. Have a look at each person's fingerprint and see how different they are from each other. Even our own fingerprints are different on each finger. To see this the children could take a print of each finger in turn and place it on a piece of paper of their own. It is amazing to think that God has given each finger on every person a different print and, if necessary, our fingerprints can identify us to others. Use this idea to thank God for making us all different, unique. Thank him that each of us is special to him, and he loves us and cares for us so much. For example:

Dear Lord, thank you that I'm special to you. Thank you that there's no one else like me. Thank you that you care for me as if I'm the only person in the world. Amen.

Songs could be sung in support of the theme. The following are suggestions:

Songs

Behold what manner of love (*JP*)
I am fearfully and wonderfully made (*SOFK*)
I'm accepted (*SOFK*)
I'm getting to know God as my Dad (*SOFK*)
I'm special (*JP*)
I'm very glad of God (*JP*)
Jesus, you love me (*SOFK*)
Lord, do I really know you? (*SOFK*)
My Lord is higher (*JP*)
Whether you're one (*JP*)

65. Getting to know God

How do we get to know someone? By spending time with them. When we see children with their friends we see them playing, talking, going round to each other's houses, sharing meals, sleeping over, sharing confidences. Isn't this how it should be in our relationship with God? We get to know him by spending time with him. How do children spend time with God?

They can do this with others in church or in their Sunday group. They can do this with a friend and they can do it on their own. The prayer ideas in this book are all about spending time with God in all sorts of places, doing many kinds of activities. One special activity is reading the Bible and spending some time with God talking about what we have read. The Bible is God's revealed word to us. God speaks to us through the Bible.

What you need

A Bible and Bible reading notes
Pen, pencil, crayons (if required)

Using the idea

Encourage your children to read their Bibles and to talk to God as if they were talking to their best friend. To help them with their Bible reading choose a version that is suitable for their age and reading ability. There are some excellent Bibles around for young children, with lots of pictures and simple text. For older children, both the Good News Bible and the New International Version are available in children's versions, as are others. It is preferable to have the text in modern language and, if using Bible reading notes, these are often based on a particular version of the Bible, so you may want to use the same one.

There are many Bible reading notes on the market. A visit to your local Christian bookshop will enable you to see those available and to choose the ones that best suit your children. Older children may like to come with you and choose for themselves. Some Bibles have suggested activities in the text.

It is good to have a set time each day for Bible reading. For many children this is at bedtime. You will probably share this time with younger children, but older children may want to do this by themselves. If this is the case, you could ask them from time to time how it is going or talk about what they have found out.

If the children are using Bible reading notes, these usually have a plan for using this time with God. After reading the Bible and the notes, then doing the activities, the children are encouraged to pray. Suggestions for this will often be given. Of course, talking to God does not have to be limited to this time. We can talk to God at any time and anywhere.

ADDITIONAL IDEA

Special place

The children might like to find a special place to meet with God. For example, under a tree in the garden. Some children we have known have used the den under their bed or the shed in the garden. The children who used their shed also invited other children to join them for Bible study.

Songs

Be still and know that I am God (*JP*)
Come on, let's go exploring (*SOFK*)
Have you got an appetite? (*SOFK*)
Isaiah heard the voice of the Lord (*JP*)
Make the book live to me, O Lord (*JP*)
My God shall supply all my needs (*SOFK*)
The best book to read is the Bible (*JP*)

66. Is God speaking?

The story of Samuel is a good illustration of how God speaks to us and also that he will speak to children, if they want him to (Samuel 3). For us to hear God we need to be available. That means we must give time to God. We must stop what we are doing and listen. But how will we know it is God and how will he speak?

What you need

A willingness to hear and some time

Using the idea

First of all the children need to know that God will speak to them. Then they need to know how – that God speaks through his word, through circumstances, and when we pray. Invite the children to ask God to speak when they read their Bibles and pray. They may feel that a verse of the Bible is an answer to their prayers. Some words or a picture may come into their mind as they pray. Get them to write this down or to tell you. It may not be clear what this is about at first, but the children can ask God what it means or who it's for. This was nine-year-old Ashley's experience in one of our Sunday groups. While we were waiting on the Lord, he had a picture. He shared this with the group, but no one knew quite what God was saying through it. We all went away and prayed about it during the week. By the time we next met, the Lord had shown Ashley what it was about.

Through these experiences, the children are learning that they may need to listen to God some more. They also need to know that we don't always hear God clearly, so we need to check the word or the picture with others. Eight-year-old Elizabeth wrote down what the Lord was saying to her and when this was shared with our vicar he told us that he already had the first part of what was a pro- phetic word for the church. This was confirmation for both of them that God was speaking and the word was shared with the church.

Children may have the gift of speaking in tongues and we can expect interpretation if a tongue is given to the church. This is less likely to happen if the adults in the church are not comfortable with the gifts of the Spirit being used, but may happen in a Sunday group with leaders who are encouraging children to ask God to use them in this way.

Songs

God is here, God is present (*SOFK*)
God is raising up an army (*SOFK*)
Let God speak (*SOFK*)

67. Journalling

Writing down what we have said to God or what God has said to us is a good way to record our prayers. It is faith-building, whatever our age, to see God answering our prayers, and when we look back through our journal, we can be encouraged to see God working in our lives and in the lives of others.

What you need

A notebook (a hardback book suggests permanence)
Pen or pencil

Using the idea

Journalling can be done at any time, but more usually after the children have read their Bibles and turned to the Lord in prayer. The children may begin their prayers based on what the Lord has been saying through the Bible reading and this may lead into intercession. To journal, encourage the children to write down their prayers in their prayer journal. They could make a column to tick when their prayers have been answered. Encourage them to ask the Lord to speak to them (see Idea 66), to listen to God and then to write down anything that comes into their mind. They can also write down any Bible verse that has spoken to them.

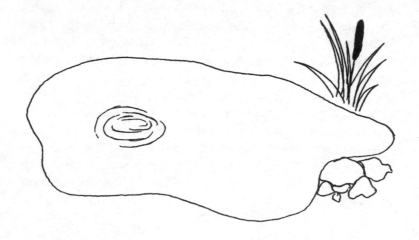

68. Ripples – or the effect of our lives on others

Have you ever thrown a pebble into a river and seen the ripples spread across the water? Our lives can be a bit like the pebble. We have an effect on the lives of others around us.

What you need

A pebble and a bowl of water

Using the idea

Drop a pebble into a bowl of water (or if you are outdoors, a river or pond) and see the water ripple outwards. Tell the children that the pebble is a bit like them. They affect others by the things they say and do. The children can use this idea to pray about their lives.

Dear Lord, please help my life to have a good effect on others. I want to tell people about you. I want to care for people like you. I want to help people like you. I want to be a good friend like you. Please help me. Amen.

Songs

A little in the hands of Jesus (*SOFK*)
I am a C (*SOFK*)
I am a lighthouse (*SOFK*)
Holy Spirit, fill me now (*SOFK*)
Keep me shining, Lord (*JP*)
This little light of mine (*JP*)

69. Hopes and fears

God is our Father and he cares about all we do. He already knows how we feel. He knows our hopes and our fears, and he is delighted when we talk to him about them.

What you need

Hopes: pen and paper
Fears: clean stone

Using the idea

The children can write down all their hopes on a piece of paper. This list can then be committed to the Lord by being placed in their Bibles (rather like being hidden in God) as you or they pray that the Lord will take care of their dreams and lead them gently onwards in their lives.

The stone can represent fears. Give each child a clean stone. Ask them to hold it tightly in the palm of their hand and to think about the things that make them afraid. Maybe it is anxiety about changing school, or decisions over which school to go to. This may be a fear of the unknown. They may feel angry or jealous. Maybe they didn't get into the school team when they thought they deserved a place. The intensity of these feelings may create fear within them. They may fear the worst about an operation. Whatever the fear, as they hold the stone, encourage them to admit their fear, then to give it to Jesus by washing the stone, burying it or, if you live by a river or the sea, you could take the child to throw their stone into the water. As they do this the prayer could be:

Lord, I'm using the stone to give to you all my fears, my worries and anxieties. I'm washing it [burying it, throwing it in the river] to show that they have gone. I trust you with my future and I ask you to take care of me and to protect me. Amen.

Songs

Do not worry (*SOFK*)
Hold on to the promises of God (*SOFK*)
I once was frightened (*SOFK*)
I do not know what lies ahead (*JP*)

70. Snooker balls

This idea came to one of our youth leaders while watching a game of snooker on the television – ideas come at the most unexpected times! It is about being right with God. The red snooker balls represent us, and the coloured balls represent feelings that can affect us. The white cue ball is the thing that triggers the response in us. The triangle represents the Trinity: God as Father, Son and Holy Spirit. This idea particularly appeals to older children who like playing snooker – especially if they can play the game first!

What you need

A set of snooker balls and a triangle

Small snooker table (optional)

Using the idea

Place the red snooker balls in the triangular frame. Explain that each ball represents a part of our lives, like being born, being a baby, being a toddler, going to pre-school, primary school, secondary school, eighteenth birthday, learning to drive, getting married (there are fifteen balls in total to label as a stage of life).

Introduce the coloured balls. These stand for feelings that can affect us, like fear, anger, loneliness, sadness, disappointment (there are seven of these). The white ball represents the trigger for these feelings.

This can be set out on a small snooker table or on the floor. (Make sure you have some kind of perimeter to keep the balls confined to one area.) Lift the triangle and roll the coloured balls in to scatter the red balls. The cue ball could be used to knock the coloured balls into the red balls. Liken this to how we feel out of sorts when we are affected by these different feelings and how we need to get ourselves back into the triangle to be in right formation again. The triangle represents God, the points of which are Father, Son and Holy Spirit. The triangle reminds us of being safe in God.

Heavenly Father, we're sorry we do things that hurt other people when we are feeling angry or sad. Help us to talk to you about how we are feeling and to think about being safe in the triangle of your love. Amen.

Songs

God loves you (*SOFK*)
Jesus loves me! (*JP*)

71. Forgive me

Saying 'sorry' is part of our relationship with God but may not always be easy. Like grown-ups, children can find it hard to say 'sorry' to others and may find it just as hard to say 'sorry' to God. One way for them to do this is to use a symbol, for example a twig, to represent the things they have done or not done, said or not said that would make God sad; or to write these things down and then throw the paper in a bin.

Symbol

What you need

A twig, a flower, a cross

Using the idea

Give each child a twig and ask them to think about something they know they need to say 'sorry' to God about. When they are ready, ask them to take the twig to the cross and, when there, to say 'sorry' as they symbolically give the twig to God. Tell them that in doing this they are owning up to what they have done wrong and asking God to forgive them. God wants us to own up to our sin and he is willing to forgive.

To help the children receive God's forgiveness, have a flower for them to pick up. This can be real or a cut-out flower with a Bible verse written on it.

If this idea is being used in a church service, and your church would normally say a prayer of confession followed by the absolution, the giving of the twig can be done as part of the confession and the picking up of the flower can be linked to the absolution.

Make it clear that the children's prayers are between them and God, and do not have to be said out loud.

Put it in the bin

What you need

Paper, pens, a bin, a cross (optional)

Using the idea

The children can write down the things they want to say 'sorry' for. When they have finished, they can take these to a bin at the foot of the cross (or just a bin), screw up the paper and throw it in the bin. If the bin is fireproof, the papers can be burned as part of this exercise – the burning being a symbolic gesture of cleansing and removing sin – but attention needs to be given to fire safety. It may be worth noting here that burned paper can leave a lingering smell in the building, as we have discovered! However, this idea does have a dramatic effect on the children and is memorable. This idea is more suitable for older children. If you don't burn the pieces of paper, you can seal them all in a rubbish bag and tell the children you will burn them at home. They need to know that no one is going to be looking at what they have written.

The children have owned up to their sin through writing it down and this they have taken to the cross (to Jesus). Pray that the children will know God's forgiveness.

Father, thank you that you have said that when we confess our sin you will forgive us and cleanse us. May we receive your forgiveness now. We ask you, Holy Spirit, to come and strengthen us, so that we don't keep doing these things we know to be wrong. In Jesus' name. Amen.

Songs

Cleanse me from my sin, Lord (*JP*)
God forgave my sin (*SOFK*)
Grace is (*SOFK*)
Jesus, you love me (*SOFK*)
One step towards Jesus (*SOFK*)
Search me, O God (*JP*)

72. Bearing fruit

How does God want us to be? Galatians 5:22–26 gives us the answer. God wants us to be loving, joyful, peaceful, patient, kind, good, faithful and full of humility and self-control. These qualities are listed as the fruit of the Spirit, and this idea is about taking these fruits and asking God to make us like each one.

What you need

Twig in a pot of soil
9 fruit-shaped pieces of paper
Felt-pens
Ribbon or wool for loops
Sticky tape

Using the idea

Write a different fruit of the Spirit on each fruit shape, colour in or decorate as required, attach a loop to each with the sticky tape and hang it on the twig. The children take it in turns to take a fruit from the tree. As they do so, they ask the Lord to make them like that fruit. For example:

> *Lord Jesus, help me to be kind to other people. Amen.*

> *Dear Lord, please help us to love one another. Amen.*

Songs

Colours of day (*JP*)
God so loved the world (*JP*)
Holy Spirit, fill me now (*SOFK*)
I am a lighthouse (*JP*)
I want to be a tree that's bearing fruit (*SOFK*)
Love, joy, peace and patience (*JP*)

73. Praying with a parachute

Most children enjoy games with a parachute or playchute, and this idea takes one game and uses it in prayer. Having tried this, the children may suggest other ways that the parachute could be used.

What you need

A parachute or playchute
6 lightweight balls
Paper and pens or pencils
Sticky tape

Using the idea

Divide the children into six groups and give each group a small piece of paper. Ask the children to write down ideas for prayer on the pieces of paper. When they have done this, stick each piece of paper onto a ball. Play a few of the children's favourite parachute games and then put the balls onto the parachute and bounce them around until one falls off. Stop the game and use the prayer idea stuck onto the ball for prayer. After praying, play again in the same way until all the balls have come off the parachute and the prayers have been prayed.

Suggested ideas

- Prayers of thanksgiving, saying 'sorry', asking for things for self/for others.
- Prayers about home: Mum, Dad, brothers, sisters, friends.
- Prayers about school: tests, learning tables, homework, friends, school trip, teachers.
- Prayers for children of other nations.
- Prayers about news items.

SECTION 8: CREATION

In the beginning God created the heavens and the earth.
(Genesis 1:1, NIV)

God wants us to enjoy his creation and he wants us to care
for all that he has made. Appreciating God's creation is his
gift for all of us, and how we care for it is our gift to future
generations. Looking at the passages in Genesis and references throughout the Scriptures to creation heightens our
marvelling at all that God has done.

'God created . . .' What does that say to us? To me it says
that he had fun, for he saw that it was good. He enjoyed
what he was making and he was encouraged by all that he
saw. He breathed life into his creation. He is a God of
movement, of activity and of stillness and rest. We read
about God creating the heavens and the earth in Genesis 1
and 2.

74. Fruit bowls

Fruit bowls are very inviting, aren't they? Actually eating the fruit is possibly the best part for a child, but many of us have a bowl of fruit on the table or worktop because simply seeing it gives us pleasure. If it didn't, the fruit may just as well be stored in the vegetable rack, don't you think? So, before we eat it, let's see what we can do with it to help us pray.

What you need

Different fruit in a bowl
A knife and cutting board suitable for the age of the children
A fruit salad bowl (optional)

Using the idea

Look at the fruit in the fruit bowl. Notice the different shapes, sizes and colours and how good they look together. Talk about this and then choose one fruit to cut in half – for example, an apple. As these are more difficult to cut, you could cut this, then together with the children look at the design. Look at the pips and ask: 'Why are they there?'

Talk about where the stalk would have been and how this held it onto the tree. Maybe you have an apple tree in the garden that the children can look at to see the apples growing. You may want to compare this with other fruits – for example, a pear (quite similar) and a banana (very different). What about strawberries, raspberries, kiwi fruit, pineapples, melons, oranges, star fruit . . .? The list is as long as the contents of your fruit bowl.

After washing their hands, the children can join you in finding out what's inside the fruit and how it is arranged. Soft fruit is easy to cut and clementines are easy to peel and divide into segments. The fruit can then be eaten, and the taste and texture of each individual fruit appreciated, or it can be placed into a salad bowl to make a fruit salad. Making a fruit salad can tap into the child's creativity if, after cutting up the fruit, they arrange it attractively in the bowl.

If you need juice for your fruit salad, I find the easiest way is to open a tin of pineapple in natural juice and tip this into the bowl and then add the other fruit to the pineapple. Alternatively, you can use any fruit juice of your choice and pour this over the fruit. You could keep some fruit for decorating, but bear in mind the colour and how well the fruit will keep when in contact with the air. Some people dip the fruit in lemon juice to overcome this problem. I usually place apple slices with the skin uppermost to protect the fleshy part from turning brown and I would do this with all fruit where the skin is to be left on. Oranges, kiwi fruit, melons and pineapples are fine. Bananas are best not left for too long in a fruit salad. Strawberries and grapes add wonderful colour.

As you look at the fruit, appreciating with the children the different sizes, colours, textures and tastes, include God in your and their discoveries.

Thank you, Lord, for hiding pips inside the fruit so that new apple trees can grow. Wow, Lord, look at all those pips inside a melon! How many melon trees might that be? I love the taste of strawberries, especially with cream. Thank you for making such nice things for us to eat. Amen.

ADDITIONAL IDEAS

Plant seeds

Try planting some of the seeds and watching to see if they will grow.

Pray for the countries from which the more exotic fruits come

Pray for the people there, the children who eat melons all the time, the fruit growers and fruit pickers. Pray that there will be enough rain in these countries for the fruit to grow well. You could find out more about the countries and what these fruits need or what happens to the fruit after it is picked.

75. Can I climb that tree?

Trees are good for climbing or for sitting under with a book. They make good hiding places when playing hide and seek. They make good homes for squirrels and birds, and they come in different shapes and sizes. They take a long time to grow and some trees live for hundreds of years. God created trees to breathe in the carbon dioxide that we breathe out and to breathe out the oxygen that we breathe in. They are important for our existence, and God knew this. This idea thanks God for trees.

What you need

A visit to a wood
Blindfolds (optional)

Using the idea

Take the children to a wood. Divide them into pairs and either blindfold one of each pair or ask them to close their eyes. Have their partner choose a tree and carefully lead them to it. The children then touch the tree. They feel the bark and hug the tree to see if their fingers will meet around the tree. When they have finished feeling the tree, their partners carefully lead them back to where they started. Remove the blindfolds, or tell them they can open their eyes, and ask them to find their tree.

Change over so both children have a turn, then talk about how they found their tree. What were they thinking about when they looked for it?

God made trees and there are many different kinds. Some have thin trunks, some fat trunks. Some bark is smooth, some is rough. Some trees have big branches, some trees have big leaves. Some leaves stay on the trees during the winter. Let's thank God for trees.

Dear Lord, thank you that every tree is different. Amen.

Creator God, thank you for big trees. Their branches look so strong and make good homes for squirrels and birds. Thank you that trees breathe out what we need to breathe in. Thank you that their roots go deep into the soil to enable them to tower high above us. They are good for climbing too! Thank you for making trees. Amen.

ADDITIONAL IDEAS

Bark rubbings

The children could take bark rubbings of their tree.

What you need

Wax crayons and paper

Using the idea

Place the paper on the bark of the tree and rub the wax crayon over it. A rubbing of the bark will appear on the paper. The children can take this home with them to remind them of their tree. They could also collect a leaf and this could be displayed with the bark rubbing. Written prayers could be added if they wish.

Count the rings

If you come across a freshly cut tree stump, try counting the growth rings to see how old the tree was. Stopping to listen to the birds singing or the wind rustling in the trees, or to look for animal tracks or at the bluebells in the wood, can bring about more appreciation of the forest.

Thank you, Lord, that this tree has been standing for so long. Thank you for the shelter that it has given to many animals and plants. Thank you that we can enjoy the woods that you have made. Amen.

76. Rest and stillness

God created the earth and by the seventh day he had finished, so he took a rest. What does it mean to rest? This idea helps the children to feel what it is like to be still.

What you need

A space big enough for active games

Using the idea

After an active game, get the children to lie down on the floor and relax. To do this, you could play the game Dead Lions, where the children have to stay as still as possible. If you want to make this competitive, you call a child out if they move, and you see who can lie still for the longest time. Some children are very good at doing this, so the game can go on for a long time! As they lie there, you could bring the children's attention to their breathing. This will be heavy to begin with, after their exertion, but it will gradually return to steady breathing. The children can be helped to appreciate the rest!

You can also compare the activity of the previous games with the stillness of this game and talk about God being busy when he made the earth and how, when he had finished, he rested. Allow this to lead into prayer, thanking God for busy times and for times to rest. The children can thank God for weekends and holidays. Older children may want to thank God for being able to lie in!

Thank you, Lord, that we can rest when we are tired.
Thank you that we are not always working hard. Amen.

ADDITIONAL IDEA

Sunday – a holy day

Talk about Sundays and why this day is different – a day of rest, a holy day. What do you do on a Sunday that makes it different? What does 'rest' mean? Does it always mean that you sit and do nothing all day? Can 'rest' mean relaxing by doing something different, like family outings, visits to the park, bike rides together or visiting grandparents or family friends? What about Sunday being a holy day? The children will be able to tell you that this is why we meet together to worship God. God knows that we need a day when we can meet with other Christians to worship him, to hear his word, to pray together and to have this special time with him.

Lord Jesus, please help us to keep Sunday special. Help us to choose things to do that give us the rest and refreshment that you intended. Help us to make time to go to church. Amen.

Songs

Be still and know that I am God (*JP*)
Be still for the presence of the Lord (*SOFK*)
I'll be still (*JP*)

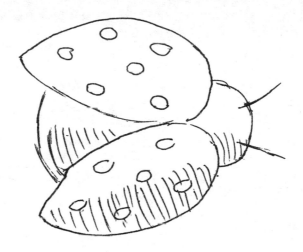

77. Ladybirds

Most children love ladybirds. They will catch them on their finger and proudly show them to you. They often have a fascination for other insects too!

What you need

Smooth pebbles, red and black poster paint, paint brush
Newspaper for covering table
Varnish or PVA glue to varnish (optional)

Using the idea

Choose a smooth pebble and paint it red. Leave it to dry

and then add black spots, face, etc. Paint with varnish or PVA glue when dry. The children now have their very own ladybird and this can remind them, when they are praying, to thank God for ladybirds and other insects and small creatures.

Dear Lord, thank you that you made ladybirds and all the insects and other very small creatures and for the place they have in your creation. Amen.

Song

If I were a butterfly (*JP*)

78. The seasons

The festivity of summer, with its hot, sunny days and outdoor activity (playing in the garden or the park, going on holiday) passes into autumn (a time of dragging your feet through the dead leaves, watching squirrels collecting nuts) in preparation for winter (a time of resting and seeming quiet but, underneath, a lot of hidden activity) and then spring (a time for new growth and for getting outside again with new things to do). The seasons are a prayer idea for older children. The idea could be used as a whole or split over four sessions – one session for each season.

What you need

Summer: flags, ribbons, music, instruments (as preferred), flower-shaped paper, pens, lolly sticks (available from craft shops), sticky tape and soil in a pot

Autumn: leaf-shaped paper, pens, branch and soil in a pot, red cloth

Winter: Bibles, Bible reading notes (optional)

Spring: Cress seeds and damp tissue paper

Using the idea

The seasons can be used to think about the rhythms of life. Children's bodies go through growth spurts. All of a sudden, or so it seems, none of their clothes fit them! In a way, our lives go through seasons too. There are growth spurts, times for sorting out problems, times to rest and times for starting something new.

Summer

Begin by praising God using flags, ribbons, dance, singing and instruments. This can be likened to the season of summer. Move into prayers of thanksgiving. Give each of the children a flower-shaped piece of paper and ask them to write down the things for which they would like to say 'thank you' to God. The children could start their prayer: 'Thank you, God, for ...'

Attach the flower shape to a lolly stick and, after they have prayed their prayer, ask the children to push these into a flowerpot filled with soil.

Autumn

Get the children to write down on a leaf-shaped piece of paper a prayer saying 'sorry' for the wrong things they have done. This prayer could begin: 'Lord Jesus, I'm sorry for ...'

When the children have prayed their prayer, ask them to place their leaves at the foot of the 'tree' – a small branch pushed into some soil in a pot. This can be likened to the leaves falling off a tree in autumn. We are giving our wrong-doings or wrong attitudes to God. The leaves could be covered with a red cloth as you tell the children that when they own up to the things they have done wrong, Jesus forgives them. It is why he died on the cross and that is why the leaves have been covered by a red cloth. Tell the children that, just as the trees have shed their leaves, they have shed their wrongdoings. This may also be a time to pray about any worries or concerns that the children may have. You could do this together or in small groups.

Winter

The next season is winter. The days are shorter and colder. The children probably spend more time indoors. Many animals hibernate, but for trees and plants a lot of activity is going on. The roots of trees are growing deeper into the soil and for some plants their roots are dividing to form new plants. In our spiritual lives, this can be the time for getting to know our Bibles a bit more. You could use the parable of the house built on sand and the house built on rock (Luke 6:46–49). This could be dramatised, or you could use *Telling Tales* (CPAS) for an all-age interactive approach. The idea is to encourage children to read their Bibles (looking at Bible reading notes could be helpful if the children don't already use them), so you could pray:

> *Lord Jesus, please help us to want to learn more about you. Help us to make time to read our Bibles and to learn more about you. Amen.*

Spring

Spring is a time for new life. Plant cress seeds on damp

tissue paper and watch them grow. Ask the children what they are looking forward to doing. Pray for each child. If you are working with a large group of children, you may want to divide the children into smaller groups or even, if the children are used to praying for each other, into twos, with each child praying for their partner. For example:

Dear Lord, please help [Darren] to play cricket really well this season so that he can make the school team. Amen.

Songs

Don't build your house (*SOFK*)
I am the apple of God's eye (*SOFK*)
I have hidden your word (*SOFK*)
I'm gonna say my prayers (*SOFK*)
In the stars his handiwork I see (*JP*)
I want to be a tree that's bearing fruit (*SOFK*)
Search me, O God (*JP*)
Thank you Lord for this fine day (*JP*)
When I look at the trees (*SOFK*)

79. Green issues

Many children have a real concern about green issues and what we are doing to the environment. If this is so for your children, take the lead from them. It may be in response to a television news item, a project at school or a leaflet picked up at the library.

What you need

Books, leaflets, posters, television news, the children's passion

Using the idea

Children may be quite passionate about environmental issues. They are having an effect on the thinking of adults by checking whether spray cans are CFC-free and prefer-ably pump action; by encouraging recycling, the use of unleaded petrol, the eating of free range eggs and dolphin-friendly tuna; by rejecting over-packaging; by following the dog with a pooper-scoop; and showing concern for rain-forests, air quality, etc. They may want to go further by making posters to display their concerns, setting up an alu-minium-can collection point or adopting a whale.

This is prayer in action. Talk about their interests and let them tell you why they are concerned about the cutting down of the rainforest, protecting endangered species, the state of our rivers, pollution in the sea or the quality of the air we breathe. Then pray together. God has put us in charge of the earth and we have a God-given responsibil-ity to care for it (Genesis 9:2).

The children can tell God about their concerns and worries, but they may also want to say 'sorry' to God on behalf of mankind because people have not cared for the earth in the way they should. For example:

Lord Jesus, please forgive us for the way we treat the earth you have made. Sometimes we've made mistakes, Lord, because we didn't know the harm we were doing, but we do know now. Please help us all to do our part in caring for everything you have made so that you can say again: 'It is good.' Amen.

Dear Lord, please forgive us for the way we allow our rivers to pollute the seas and, in turn, to pollute beaches even on the other side of the world, affecting wildlife, fish and other creatures and plants in the sea. Help us as

*a nation to take more care of the country you have
given to us to look after and more care of the sea. Amen.*

Prayers may be for groups trying to bring about changes in
attitudes and behaviour, or for children as they help their
families to think about how they can be more environmen-
tally friendly.

80. Creatures great and small

Big animals, small animals, animals that can swing through trees, animals that scurry through the undergrowth, animals with long necks, animals in the jungle, animals on the farm, animals in our homes. God commanded: '"Let the earth produce all kinds of animal life: domestic and wild, large and small"... and he was pleased with what he saw' (Genesis 1:24–25).

Most children love being around animals. This can be at the zoo, the safari park, the working farm or at home. This love of animals can take prayers in many directions, from giving thanks to God for making animals, to praying for protection of endangered species or for animals that have been mistreated.

What you need

Contact with animals at home or through visits to the zoo, safari park or working farm
Pictures in books or magazines
Television or videos

Using the idea

Most children want a pet, and if they are able to have one it is a good way for them to learn about animals and how to care for them – to be responsible for feeding the pet, keeping it clean and exercised, and cuddling it, if appropriate! As the children care for their pet, they are fulfilling Proverbs 12.10 which says: 'A good man takes care of his animals.'

The children can thank God for their pet. For example:

Lord Jesus, thank you for making rabbits. I like watching [Bobtail] hop about and I like holding him. I can tell him all my secrets and he won't tell anyone else. He's good company. Please keep him safe. Amen.

ADDITIONAL IDEAS

Visit to the zoo or safari park

Visiting the zoo or safari park may help children to see animals they wouldn't normally see in this country. The children may look forward to going. Some children may look forward to seeing the animals but have concerns about them being kept in captivity. This issue can be talked over and prayed about. Some species are only surviving because of the breeding programmes in zoos. It may help the children to know this and that some animals are being bred with the aim of returning them to the wild.

Visit to a working farm

On working farms children can often help to milk cows. They can stroke donkeys and make friends with sheep. As they explore the farm, you could marvel with them and help them to turn their delight into prayers of thanksgiving. For example:

> *Thank you, God, for cows that give us milk. For their big eyes and soft nose. Thank you that they come to the gate each morning and evening to be milked and that they look happy eating grass in the fields. Be with the farmers who look after them. Amen.*

Watch a video

We have videos telling the adventures of various animals. These range from dogs and a cat to whales, a seal and a baby panda. These give ideas for prayer. The children may want to pray about the dangers for the animals, like an oil spillage or hunters. This might be especially relevant if they were hearing about it on the television news.

Adopt an animal

Watching videos like these or visiting the zoo, the safari park or the working farm can also give them ideas for adopting their favoured animal!

Songs

Have you seen the pussycat? (*SOFK/JP*)

He made the earth (*SOFK*)
If I were a butterfly (*SOFK/JP*)
Mister Cow (*SOFK*)
Mister Noah built an ark (*JP*)
There once was a shepherd (*SOFK*)
Think of a world without any flowers (*JP*)

81. What's the weather doing?

Is it raining? Will it be hot today? Do you want it to snow? Are we ever happy with our weather? How can we use the weather in our prayers?

What you need

Today's weather

Using the idea

1. It's really hot today

Would you like a drink? What would it be like if there

wasn't any water in the tap; if you didn't have a tap and the well had dried up; if the rivers and streams had dried up? Use this to pray for people in countries that are experiencing drought.

2. It's wet and windy today

That means you can't go out to play, but what is it like outside in this weather? What would it be like if you had no home to go back to? Pray for the homeless and the street children. Thank God for your own home, for food and warm, dry clothes.

3. Can you see the rainbow?

What makes it? How many colours can you see? The children could find out from Genesis 9:11–16 that it is a reminder of God's promise to us. Use this to thank God for his promise.

ADDITIONAL IDEA

Television news

The television news may tell you about rivers flooding, an earthquake, forest fires, a landslide, thick smog making breathing difficult for the people caught up in it, etc. Use these news items to pray for the people and wildlife caught up in these disasters.

Songs

Have you heard the raindrops? (*JP*)
It's a happy day (*SOFK*)
Who put the colours in the rainbow? (*SOFK*)

82. Hidden in the dark

What's under the stone? What lives in the soil? What do
they eat? Do they bite? Why don't they get squashed? Can
they breathe? Young children usually like hunting for small
creatures under leaves or stones and looking at them
through magnifying glasses or in bug catchers. Older children may like to make a wormery to see how the earthworms tunnel through the soil.

Earthworms

What you need

Moist soil or potting compost

Moist sand
A transparent, wide-mouthed container or jar
Kitchen peelings
Dark paper or thick newspaper to wrap around the jar
Sticky tape
4 or 5 earthworms

Using the idea

Layer the soil and sand. Place the peelings on top and put
the earthworms on the peelings. Cover the sides of the container with the paper, sticking it down with the tape. Leave
the jar for a week, except for adding more peelings and
checking that the soil stays moist. After a week, take the
paper away and see how the worms have tunnelled through
the soil. The food they have been eating fertilises the soil.
The work of the earthworm goes on in the hidden depths
of the soil, but it is vital for the health of the soil. Knowing
this makes us want to thank God for paying attention to
such details in his creation.

> *Worms are such funny creatures, Lord. They are made
> up of so many segments that even when cut in half they
> can still live. Thank you that you made them to be
> happy eating the soil and living in the dark. Thank you
> for the hidden work that you are doing in the soil that
> is necessary for the plants to grow. Thank you for the
> details of your creation. Amen.*

Other creatures

If the children are discovering the homes of woodlice,
snails or millipedes, they can pray for these and their place
within God's creation. There are so many little creatures to
find – not only in the garden, but on the seashore or along

the riverbank. What's under the sand? Ask the children if they can see signs on the beach when the tide has gone out. Some people collect the creatures under the sand. Fishermen dig into the sand to find lugworms for bait. The children will be interested in other small creatures on the rocks and in the rock pools. Were any of these hiding? What about shells? Are creatures living in these? Praise God for making so many different creatures to live in hidden places.

Songs

He made the earth (*SOFK*)
If I were a butterfly (*SOFK/JP*)

83. Did you catch anything?

Do you remember going down to the pond or the canal with your bucket and fishing net to see what you could catch? Sticklebacks were the most common, I remember, with a beetle or two! Younger children delight in their catch. Older children delight too, but they may prefer to fish with a rod and line. All these fish can be returned to the water when the children have looked at them. Another place to see fish is at one of the Sealife Centres. Pet shops and zoos often have tanks of fish too.

What you need

Fishing net and bucket

Using the idea

Go fishing. Watch the fish swim around. Are they on their own or with others? The children can try to catch some in their net (this activity needs adult supervision). Put the fish in the bucket and when the children have finished their fishing, have a look at them. Are all the fish the same? How do they breathe? What do they eat? Empty the fish back into the water.

The children can thank God for making fish to swim in the water. They can either do this while they are out, as a natural part of the fishing trip, or they can do it later if they prefer to pray at home. The prayer could be written on a fish-shape piece of paper, or fish shapes could be made into a mobile.

After a visit to a Sealife Centre or aquarium, the prayer might be:

Creator God, thank you that you made fish to swim in the water. Fish of all different sizes and colours. Some fish to live in cold water and other fish to live in warm water. Fish to eat and fish to keep in aquaria. Fish to be wary of, like sharks, sting-rays and some jellyfish. Help us to care for the water that the fish live in. May we do what we can to keep it clean. Amen.

ADDITIONAL IDEAS

Fish in rock pools

If you are near a beach, fishing in rock pools is fun. What can you find? You may find sea anemones, barnacles, periwinkles, seaweed, small crabs or even small fish. It is exciting to find so many different things. Thank God for all that he has made.

Fish in the Bible

If you want to develop this one, you could look at the references to fish in the Bible. For example:

- Calling of the first disciples (Luke 5:1–11);
- Jesus feeds the five thousand (Matthew 14:13–21);
- Jesus and the miraculous catch of fish (John 21:1–14);
- Jonah swallowed (Jonah 1) and prayer (Jonah 2).

Prayers would follow as appropriate to the Bible readings.

Songs

5,000 + hungry folk (*SOFK*)
Big man (*SOFK*)
Come listen to my tale (*JP*)
What a whale of a tale (*SOFK*)
Who took fish and bread? (*JP*)

84. Through the eyes of a mouse

We have a shed in the lower part of our small split-level garden, and it has a window that looks out over our upper garden, giving a ground-eye view. The soil is at eye level, and you can see the flower stalks. If you look upwards, you see the under sides of the flowers. It is darker than in the garden because the plants bring shadow – they hide what is below. Looking out, the view is that of a mouse. Imagine that world. As a mouse, you can scurry around, protected by the cover of the plants. This idea uses the children's imaginations and the height of plants and vegetation to see the world in a slightly different way.

What you need

A split-level garden/piece of ground or a cellar window
Vegetation that is taller than the children

Using the idea

Using the mouse idea, you could tell the children to imagine they are a little mouse. They come out of their nest to find food. How might they feel coming into this under plant world? Do they feel safe? Your questions could consider the food mice eat, the mouse's enemies, what a mouse needs to survive.

The children may want to thank God for the protection that the taller plants give to mice and other small animals, or a prayer idea may come to them as they think about the games they have played. They may also want to thank God for looking after them.

Thank you, Lord God, that as you have a way of looking after the creatures you have made, so you look after me. Amen.

ADDITIONAL IDEAS

Indoor alternative

If the weather doesn't permit an outside activity, try this indoor alternative. Lie, crouch or crawl on the floor and look up at the furnishings. Imagine that the chairs and the tables are providing shelter and hiding places, and that the light is the sun. Ask the children to crawl or slide along the floor into a hiding place.

Games

These games are set in vegetation taller than the children.

Hide and seek

The children could be divided into two groups. One group could go together to hide. The other then tries to find them. The key here is for the first group to stay very quiet. This activity is not suitable for young children or for those who are inclined to get lost, although they can take part with adequate supervision!

Tracking

Within a defined area, one group of children could go ahead and mark a trail. They could do this with arrows made out of sticks or something similar. You could plan with them various signs – for example, two sticks made into a cross to say 'not this way' at the junction with another path. The first group need a head start, especially as they have to prepare the trail. When the trail is laid, they hide behind the trees, staying very quiet. The second group then follow the trail. It's a bit like stalking or being stalked. For safety, you may want an adult to accompany each group.

Enjoy the games and at the end sit quietly. The children can use this time to thank God for the plants, bushes and trees that he has made which provide somewhere for smaller animals to live, feed and hide.

SECTION 9: GOD'S WORK

Here am I. Send me! (Isaiah 6:8, NIV)

What better motivation for praying for God's work than doing it? It doesn't matter how old we are, each one of us can be used by God. All we need to be is willing and available. Maybe our prayer begins: 'Here I am, Lord. What would you like me to do?'

Adults in the church may be finding out what their gifts are. These can be practical as well as spiritual. This can be going on for children too. In order for children to know what their spiritual gifts are, they will need teaching on the gifts of the Spirit. They will also need the opportunity to put these gifts into practice. (See 'Children and spiritual gifts' in Part One.)

85. Being yourself

This is an important way of doing God's work as other people read the gospel according to you! How you live, how you care for others, will speak volumes. It is important to build up self-worth in children. It helps them to know that they are uniquely made by God and that they are loved and cared for by him because of who they are. By being themselves they can be doing God's work.

What you need

Pen and paper for each child
Confidence and encouragement to be themselves

Using the idea

The positives

The children could encourage one another by writing down the things they like about others in the group. Remind them that they are only to write down positive things! They could write under the heading 'I like you because ...', with comments like:

- You are kind.
- You listen.
- You help me do things I find difficult.
- You make me laugh with your jokes.
- You are understanding.
- You have a good sense of humour.

Sharing these things with each other will help to build up self-worth.

Thank you, God, for making me me

The children can be encouraged to pray that their lives will be pleasing to Jesus. They can ask God to help them to find ways to help those around them. The prayer may go something like this:

Father God, thank you for making me me. There is no one else quite like me. You have given gifts to me that are specially mine. You have given me my own life to be lived with my family and friends, those in my class at school, people in my church. Help my life to be pleasing to you. Help me to live my life for Jesus. May the things I say and do show that I belong to you. Help me to use my gifts to bring happiness to others. Thank you, Lord. Amen.

Feeling valued

Being able to do something for someone else will help them to feel valued. Talk about what the children enjoy doing. For example, they may like:

- riding their bike;
- writing stories;
- reading;
- making cakes;
- playing with Lego;
- swimming;
- football;
- playing a musical instrument.

They could think about how they can use these interests for God. Maybe, as a group, there are enough children who like playing football that a sponsored football match could be arranged, with the proceeds going to help children in another part of the world. Any of their interests could be chosen. Maybe they could befriend others by including them in their interests. Children being themselves, but with a care for others.

Songs

A little in the hands of Jesus (*SOFK*)
If I were a butterfly (*JP/SOFK*)
My God is so big (*JP*)
You may think I'm so young (*SOFK*)

86. Helping in church

God's work includes handing out books, tidying chairs, making squash, decorating the church and putting up acetates or hymn numbers. Being given a job can help children to feel part of the church. It can give them a greater interest in how the church is run.

What you need

Jobs to be done, and willing helpers to do them

Using the idea

The children will feel more valued if they are working

within a team. This can be an all-age team and the children can be included in that team for prayer. Those involved in preparing for a service can join together before the service begins to pray for those taking part and for their own part in it. For example, putting up acetates may place them within the worship team, so the children can be included in the prayer preparation of the worship group. Handing out books may place them in the welcoming team, so the children can be included in the prayer preparation of this team.

Before serving coffee, the children may want to pray:

> *Father God, we are here to serve you. Help us to do this well and in a way that will show people we care about them. Amen.*

Before welcoming people into church, a prayer might be:

> *Father God, give us smiley faces as we welcome people into church today. May they see your love for them in our welcoming. Thank you, Lord. Amen.*

Before putting up the acetates:

> *Father God, help us to listen to the worship leader and to follow where we are in the service so that we get the acetates up at the right time. We are doing this to serve you and to serve the congregation. Please help the congregation to really worship you today. Amen.*

The children can be encouraged to pray their own prayers and if they feel at all anxious about what they are going to do, they can receive encouragement through the prayers of others in the team.

ADDITIONAL IDEA

Helping someone in their home

Older children could help people in their homes. Maybe someone in the church needs help to dust the house, vacuum the carpets, clean the bath, change the bed. This can be an opportunity for the children to show that they care, and at the same time do God's work. The children can be encouraged to pray for the person. You could ask questions like: 'How were they today? Is their shoulder any better?' This can lead into praying for the person. Something like:

> *Father God, continue to bring your healing to [name]. Please take the pain away and help her shoulder to get better soon. Amen.*

Tip: If your children want to serve God in this way, be aware of your church's child protection policy. It would be better for them to go as a small group. Young teens may be able to do this by themselves. Slightly younger children may need you to stay with them and help them with the tasks.

Songs

Give me oil in my lamp (*JP*)
Jesus' hands were kind hands (*JP*)

87. Taking part in services

In some churches, children may be able to take part in services by singing, playing an instrument, being in a drama or dance, leading prayers or even by leading the service or preaching. This is another way of doing God's work and enables the church to disciple children in areas of ministry. It also enables the children to explore their gifts and to find out what God may want them to do. This can be done in various ways.

With Sunday groups

The Sunday groups could be asked to lead the service and this will provide the opportunity for the children to pray about and prepare different parts of the service. Using ideas from resources like *SALT All-Age* or talks from books like Sue Relf's *100 Instant Children's Talks* and *100 Instant Ideas for All-Age Worship* can help to get them going. Some of the older children may even feel able to give the talk. One of our children was writing five-minute talks when she was nine and gave her first talk in church at an all-age service when she was thirteen.

With a ministry team

Another way is for the children to be included with the adult ministry groups. In this way they are discipled and mentored to that particular area of ministry and are involved in the praying of that ministry team. We are exploring this with music in our church. Young musicians are invited to rehearse with the worship group for the monthly all-age service. Not all the children will play all of the time, but they will all have the opportunity to join in with one of the songs – even if they can only play a few notes! Children have also been included in a similar way in drama and dance.

What you need

A supportive leadership team in the church
Opportunity for the Sunday groups to lead services or for the children to join a ministry team

Using the idea

Whether the children are preparing for the service in their group or joining with a ministry team, it is a good opportunity for them to be praying and listening to God with the people with whom they will be working. We have a children's drama group in our church and they are encouraged to pray, to ask God to give them ideas for the drama. Each child is encouraged to listen to God. Maybe the Lord will give them a picture. The leader sets the scene by giving the children the theme and then asking God to show the group what they are to do. Their prayer together might go something like this:

> *Lord, we invite you to come and speak to us. We want this drama to be your drama – one that has come from you. In the stillness now we ask you to give us your ideas. Thank you, Lord. Amen.*

The children are given a piece of paper on which to write or draw what comes into their minds during the silence. They then share their ideas, they try them out, the leader takes the pieces of paper home and prepares a framework for the next meeting based on the children's ideas, and slowly the final drama emerges. This drama still has an element of spontaneity about it and this remains so on the day. The children are learning to trust God and one another; to keep listening to God and to each other.

If working with a ministry team, it may be easier, of course, for the drama, dance or worship leader to have prepared ideas, especially if time is short. This is fine. It must be said that it can be hard work for the ministry team to be including children, but it is worth the effort and the children will benefit from being alongside adults as they pray and prepare.

Prayers can also be for one another, asking God for his courage, his words to say, and for the anointing of his Holy Spirit for those leading. The children can pray too for the congregation or, if it is an open-air service, for those who will be passing by – that they will meet with God, that they will learn more about him and that they will allow God to touch them.

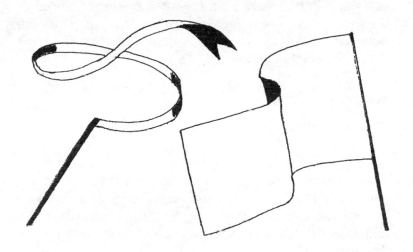

88. Declaring that we are on God's side!

Flags and ribbons are a declaration of a spiritual truth. In battle, flags show whose side we are on (e.g. Numbers 1:50 – 2:2, 17, 31, 34). The colours are symbolic and this can be explained to the children, for example: gold for majesty; purple for kingship; blue for the water of life; silver for the Holy Spirit; red for Jesus (death of Christ, sacrifice, salvation, grace); green for healing, rest, life; yellow for glory, light, celebration; black for sin and death.

Children usually enjoy using flags and ribbons! If you have open-air services they are ideal to use as they are colourful and crowd-attracting. They can also be used within the church building if there is space. They can be used spontaneously or you may want to plan movements that the children can present together as a group. The children will need to be taught how to use the flag or ribbon, both for the safety of others and so that they don't get themselves tied up in knots!

What you need

Flags and/or ribbons

To make a flag

Take a piece of lightweight material (60cm × 50cm in the colour you want). Turn over the shorter edge and sew up to make a slot for a cane 75cm long. Sew up the end of the slot and slide in the cane. Attach the flag to the cane using sticky fixers.

To make a ribbon

Take a length of double-sided satin ribbon (approximately 3m long and 5cm wide). Hem the short ends and sew one end to a ring, which is then attached to a swivel (this can be bought from a fishing shop). Screw a closed hook into the top of a piece of lightweight dowling (approximately 30cm long) and attach the swivel to the hook.

For younger children

Scale down the sizes. Wooden chopsticks with five different coloured ribbons (30cm × 1cm) make safe and attractive 'wavers' for under-fives. Similarly, small flags can be attached to the wooden chopsticks.

Choose a song

What you need

Flags and/or ribbons

Using the idea

The easiest way for using flags and ribbons is to choose a song like 'The time has come' (Mick Gisbey) and wave them as exhorted in verse 2. Any song of celebration will provide the opportunity for the children to make their declaration that they are on God's side – that God is here – and their moving of the flags and ribbons is their prayer. This may be that others will come to know Jesus, or it may be in their giving of their praise to God – a 'thank you' for all that he is and for all that he has done. Prayers don't need to be spoken. This one is moved!

Planned movements

This idea is based on 'Make Way' (Graham Kendrick) and includes some interpretive movements. This song is not in itself a prayer, but it is a testimony to the Lord we worship. It is a call to worship and a song declaring biblical truth.

What you need

Flags
A Jesus figure
Children to come forward for prayer

Using the idea

Verse 1: children enter the room carrying the flags high, as in an army marching into battle.

Chorus 1: the children form a V-shape at the front of the room with flags held high and outstretched.

Verse 2: a child representing Jesus can stand at the open end of the V-shape. Others come forward for prayer. The

Jesus figure lays hands on each child and they leave with happy faces.

Chorus 2: children with flags walk round in a circle and reform the V on 'And let his kingdom in'.

Verse 3: the Jesus figure comforts a sad child.

Chorus 3: as chorus 2.

Verse 4: Jesus figure walks through to the top of the V-shape, flags raised as he passes by.

Chorus 4: the children turn to face the congregation, standing in a large enough space to wave the flags in celebration.

The songs for both the above ideas can be found in *Songs of Fellowship for Kids*.

Using flags and ribbons safely

- Watch the flag or the ribbon and be mindful of others near you.
- A 'figure of 8' movement will prevent the flag from wrapping around the cane or the ribbon around the stick.
- The power and strength of the movements will be determined by the situation, as will the variation of movements, and may require more space.
- When children are using flags, remember that the top of the flag may be at eye level for adults!

89. Carol singing

What is carol singing? For most churches it is probably seen as a form of pre-evangelism. It is a way for the church to be noticed by the community and, in most communities, will be accepted as part of the build-up to Christmas. It is a way for the church to sing out the gospel. It is a way in which the children can be involved in God's work.

What you need

Carol sheets and musicians (if available)
A planned route
Warm clothes, hats, scarves, gloves
A torch

Using the idea

Whether the children are joining a larger church group or carol singing in their own group, before you go out gather together to pray for the people who will hear the carols. Pray that this may be a time when they stop what they are doing and think about what Christmas is really about – it is more than rushing around buying presents and planning menus.

> *Father God, help us to sing well for you. We pray that the people will hear what we are singing and will want to come to church at Christmas. We want them to know that Christmas is more than presents and parties; it's your birthday. Thank you, Lord. Amen.*

You will want to think about safety on the roads as you go carol singing and, if the group is mainly children, have enough adults to supervise adequately. Your church may like you to push leaflets through people's doors. Children can share in this. Suggest that they are careful not to push their fingers through the letter boxes, as some can catch a finger. Make sure that the children are with an adult who can account for them. It is easy to get separated in the dark. And watch out for dogs, both in people's gardens and just behind front doors.

ADDITIONAL IDEA

Mince pies

Most children enjoy baking, so why not make mince pies or something similar with them before they go carol singing and serve these with hot drinks or squash afterwards? For this you will need your favourite recipe. Yum!

90. Giving money

Doing God's work can be in the regular giving of money to a particular project or missionary group. It helps the children to respond to God when they know that they are part of his work when they give and that their giving helps others. They also need to know that God tells us in the Scriptures that we should give. All this will help them to pray for the work they are supporting, as they understand their part in the grander scheme of things.

Collecting-boxes are one way of encouraging children to give regularly. These are readily available from missionary or similar organisations. And if the one of your choice does not have collecting-boxes, you could make one!

What you need

A collecting-box from the missionary group of your choice
OR
A collecting-box you have made. Cover a small box in
shiny paper, wrapping paper or plain paper. The children
could decorate their box either by colouring their design or
attaching stickers to the box. Once the box is made, you will
need to cut a hole in the top for the money.

Using the idea

At home

For use at home, you could have a regular time each week
when the children put money in the box. The box could be
used for their tithe money as a giving box. This might be the
time for praying for the missionary group concerned. The
missionary group may also produce a prayer letter or magazine. Some have newsletters for children and these will
have ideas for prayer. Use these ideas to get you started.
Younger children can look at the pictures in the newsletter
and they too can join in praying. If your church has a link
missionary, you may want to give prayer support to that
person and receive their prayer letter.

In church

For use in church, you may want to have a box in your
group that children add money to each week, or the children could have their own boxes to take home. If the box
is in your group, decide together with your leadership team
how often you would like to include prayer for mission in
your group's programme. If the children have their boxes
at home, collect them in each term and use that session to
pray for the missionary work you support.

One of our church's link missionaries is in Tanzania, a country that was suffering famine as a result of the drought. In this kind of instance, the children may want to pray for food during the famine, and rain so that the next crop will grow. Their prayer might be:

Father God, thank you that Christians in this country are giving money to help buy food for the people in Tanzania. We pray for the churches in Tanzania as they give out the food. Help there to be enough so that no one will be hungry, and please send rain for next year's crop. Thank you, Lord. Amen.

Song

Pressed down, shaken together (*SOFK*)

91. Entertaining and visiting

The elderly particularly like to see children and this can be a good way of introducing children to people who may be lonely, giving pleasure to both. The visit may be to a residential home for the elderly or to the home of an elderly member of the church. The size of the place you are visiting will determine the number of children who can be involved. This is another way of doing God's work and of using the children's gifts.

What you need

Willing children, and people to entertain or visit

Using the idea

Entertaining

The children may like to plan this visit to include singing, reading, dancing or playing an instrument. This could be in the form of a service or as entertainment. The programme should not be too long – twenty minutes may be enough for all concerned, followed by a cup of tea and a chat.

As the children will be coming from the local church, the people they are visiting will not be surprised to have prayer included in the programme. This may be more formal if the children are leading a service, or it can be an opening or concluding prayer. For example:

Heavenly Father, we thank you for this time together. We ask now for your blessing to be upon us. In Jesus' name we pray. Amen.

The children can also be encouraged to pray for the people they have met when you are back in your group. If you visit a residential home, maybe the children could choose one of the people as their person to pray for. They could do this by writing or drawing their prayer in their prayer book, or by praying aloud in the group, or by praying with a prayer partner. If you make regular contact with the home, you may wish to have photographs of the residents on display to act as a focus for the children as they pray. If the visit is to elderly members of the church, they too may be willing to provide photographs.

Children may find it helpful to talk about what life may be like as an elderly person. This could be acted out in role-play. The children could think about how life slows down. An older person's body doesn't run and jump as their bodies do. Walking or climbing stairs may be difficult. What about going shopping? It can be lonely living on your own. This will help them to understand a little more and so give them ideas for prayer.

> *Father God, please be with [Mrs Johnson] today. Help her to be more comfortable as she moves around. May she get the relief from pain that she needs. Thank you, Lord. Amen.*

Visiting

Visiting for a chat while playing board games provides contact. If they don't know the person they are visiting, it will be easier for the children if a grown-up is with them, as this will keep the conversation going. Doing something like playing a board game gives both the child and the elderly person a focus for conversation.

Regular visiting can help develop relationships, which in turn can build up prayer links between the children and the people they visit. The children can write in their prayer books or add their prayer to the group prayer board. They could pray with the person they are visiting before they leave, and maybe that person can also pray for them. In making your arrangements, remember to take note of your church's child protection policy.

92. Calling cards

Children of any age can make calling cards for your vicar, minister, church leader or pastoral care team to take with them as they visit members of the church. The cards can be pre-printed with a picture for the children to colour; the picture could be pre-printed and, after colouring, stuck onto the card; or the children could make their own, using dried flowers, cut-out material, their own drawing, sponge painting, ink printing, etc. Making these cards is another way in which the children can take part in God's work – this time in pastoral care.

What you need

Card, pre-printed pictures or other chosen materials
Felt-pens, crayons or pencils
Glue sticks (if required)

Using the idea

While making the cards, talk about how the church shows
care by visiting. The children can share in this care by
making cards for the visitors to take with them. Think
about the greeting you may want the children to write
inside. Your church may have a preferred one and this
might even be pre-printed and stuck inside, or could be
printed directly onto A4 paper, which could then be folded
to make the card. The message might read:

> *We are praying for you.*
> *From St Andrew's Church.*
> *(Made by Jason.)*

Or:

> *The minister called today.*
> *From the Baptist church.*
> *(Made by Naomi.)*

If the card is pre-printed, a space can be left for the children to write in their name; for example:

'Made by ....'

The children could also pray for the people who will
receive the cards and for those who will take them out.

93. Making cakes

Making something for someone else can be a tangible reminder that someone is praying for them. The gift gives the message that someone has thought about them, and this can reflect God's love and care. In the making of the gift, the children are a part of God's work.

This idea uses cakes or biscuits as the gift. If you prefer, the children could decorate pebbles, make small posies of flowers, or even make flower arrangements.

What you need

Your favourite cake recipe
OR

100g (4oz) margarine
100g (4oz) sugar
100g (4oz) self-raising flour
2 eggs
Baking cases
Baking tin
Icing sugar

Method

1. Cream margarine and sugar until light and fluffy.
2. Add eggs. Beat well.
3. Stir in the flour.
4. Spoon mixture into baking cases.
5. Place in pre-heated oven (Gas mark 4; electric 180°C) for 15 to 20 minutes.
6. Cool on a cooling rack.
7. Ice and decorate as required.

For a biscuit recipe, please see Idea 9.

Using the idea

The children could write a prayer on a card to give with the cake or biscuit. The prayer could be: 'May God bless you today,' or, 'May you know more of Jesus' love for you today.'

The children may want to personalise the prayer more by using the person's name if they know who they are giving the cakes or biscuits to. The children can be encouraged to continue to pray for that person during the week. The cakes could be given out after the church service or taken to the homes of those not able to be at church that day.

SECTION 10: GOD'S WORD

Your word is a lamp to guide me and a light for my path.
(Psalm 119:105)

Children need to know the word of God so that they
know how to live a life that is pleasing to God. The word
of God will help them to get to know both God and themselves better. The Bible is a history book – a testimony to
all that God has done and to the response of his people.
It is a guidebook – telling us how to live our lives. It
brings comfort and correction. It is a weapon in spiritual
warfare.

God commanded the Israelites to tell their children all
that they had seen and heard so that they, in due course,
would do the same (Deuteronomy 4:9–14). The Jews today
continue to do this as they meet together on the eve of the
Sabbath for their family meal and as they enact the festi-
vals. Our children learn in the same way. For those growing
up in Christian families, seeing their parents reading the
word and praying, joining in family prayer and Bible times,
thanking God for his provision at mealtimes, joining with
other Christians to worship God, showing love, care and
hospitality to others, being a listening ear, giving freely of
time and money – all show the children how to live the
Christian life.

This section is about praying, knowing and understanding God's word, the Bible. Before children can pray the word they need to know it. And to know the word, they need to read it or hear it read.

94. Pray the word

Praying the word of God over people has a powerful effect. Begin with scriptures that are prayers – for example Numbers 6:24–26:

> *'May the Lord bless you and take care of you; may the Lord be kind and gracious to you; may the Lord look on you with favour and give you peace.' Amen.*

Or Philippians 4:7:

> *I pray that 'God's peace, which is far beyond human understanding, will keep your hearts and minds safe in union with Christ Jesus', Amen.*

The children can learn these or read them from their Bibles.

What you need

Bibles

Using the idea

When praying for someone it can help to place a hand gently on their shoulder. Laying on of hands is scriptural and children can be encouraged to do this, especially in prayers for healing or prayers of blessing. If touching the person is not appropriate, it can be helpful to stretch a hand towards the person receiving prayer.

Praying Scripture brings an authority to our prayers. Children can be encouraged to pray the word of God as they pray in praise, thanksgiving, confession or intercession. Help them to find an appropriate verse. The Psalms are a good source of verses. For example:

> To you, O Lord, I offer my prayer; in you, my God, I trust. (Psalm 25:1)

In praise and thanksgiving:

> Praise the Lord! Give thanks to the Lord, because he is good. (Psalm 106:1)

As they listen to God:

> Teach me your ways, O Lord; make them known to me. (Psalm 25:4)

In praying for help:

I look to the mountains; where will my help come from? My help will come from the Lord, who made heaven and earth. (Psalm 121:1–2)

The children's own prayers can follow. For example:

Lord Jesus, I am looking to you for help. I need to know how to react to my friend. She is sad and I want to know how best to help her. Please show me what to do. Amen.

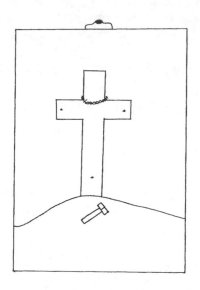

95. Focus the word

A few moments' quiet reflection *is* possible with children! We've done it, and we've been surprised how well the children have responded. Watching a candle or playing music quietly in the background can help to set an atmosphere for reflective prayer. The idea is not to manipulate the children, but to create a place where the children can be still and quiet and think about Jesus. This is a time for them to grow closer to God, to feel his presence and to listen to him. You may want to help them to do this by reading a Bible verse to focus their thoughts.

What you need

Prayer focus – for example, candle, cross, leaves, flower, snail (as relevant)
Paper and pencils

Using the idea

Quietly reflecting with children in church

It is possible to have quiet reflection with children in church. We have done this for five minutes in a church service, focusing on a candle, listening to music or watching the change of pictures on the overhead projection screen. We have also spent longer in special services, an example of which follows.

In our church we always have a special all-age service on Maundy Thursday. This is in the early evening and begins with praise and worship and leads on to enacting the events of the Last Supper, including a meal and the sharing of bread and wine. Each year this service is a little different!

One Maundy Thursday, as we returned to the church after the meal and sharing of the bread and wine in the hall, we were thinking about Jesus walking to the Garden of Gethsemane. We entered the church in silence, listening to the song 'Stay with me' (Les Presses de Taizé, France) which presented the theme and set the atmosphere. The church was in dim light with a large cross as the focal point. A crown of thorns, large nails and a lump hammer were at the foot of the cross. After a short spoken introduction based on Luke 22:24–30, in the quiet, parents took their children to the cross, where they could look up at the wooden cross, feel the weight of the nails and the hammer, touch the crown of thorns.

Some stayed there looking at the cross. Others picked up

pencils and wrote or drew their response on paper. They recorded the thoughts, pictures or poems that were coming into their minds. There was opportunity to share these later.

The church was in silence and these children from as young as three were caught up in a time with the Lord. When it came to going home, many children wanted to stay. It was getting late, but the experience of God's presence was very strong.

Quietly reflecting with children in groups

In groups, the children can focus on a cross, a candle, a leaf, a flower, an animal, or whatever focus will help the prayer time. For example, if the Bible verse is about how much Jesus cares for the lilies of the field and how much more he cares about you and me (Matthew 6:28–30), then the children could be given a flower to look at. Following the group leader's introduction, ask the children to stay quiet and think about what they have heard. Have pencils and paper available for children to write down or draw thoughts that have come into their minds. Talk about these afterwards.

Quietly reflecting with younger children

It is possible to use this idea with younger children. With three- and four-year-olds, we've developed it out of a cuddle time. This had been a time when parents or leaders have gathered the children close to them and, with gentle music playing, the children have sat quietly enjoying the cuddle and the feeling of peace. Another way is for children to lie on the floor while the music plays. The time can conclude with a prayer on the theme of the meditation. For example:

Thank you, Jesus, for your love.

Or

Thank you, Jesus, for making leaves.

For this latter idea, each child could be given a leaf to hold and to look at during the cuddle time. This could follow on from activities with leaves, like walking through leaves in the park, or painting and then printing with leaves.

The objective of this time is for the children to quieten down and to focus their thoughts on God or Jesus. This is a time for them to grow closer to God, to feel his presence and to listen to him.

96. Sing the word

What better way to learn Scripture than to sing it and then to use the scriptural song in prayer?

What you need

Songs of Fellowship for Kids or any suitable children's songbook

Using the idea

Many of the songs are based on Scripture and this may be enough for you. The children are learning scriptural truths as they sing. If you want the children to learn the reference

as well, some songs, like 'Delight yourself in the Lord –
Psalm 37 verse 4' (Ishmael), 'In Proverbs 4 it clearly says'
(Mick Gisbey) and 'We believe in Hebrews 13:8' (Ishmael),
include these in the lyrics. Other songs have the Bible references noted under the title or at the top right-hand
corner of the page to help you.

Songs with particular reference to prayer include: 'As for
me and my house' (Jim Bailey), 'Do not worry' (Doug
Horley), 'I'm gonna say my prayers' (Ishmael), 'Prayer is
like a telephone' (Paul Crouch and David Mudie), 'Teach
us, Lord, how to pray' (Mick Gisbey).

Other songs are prayers in themselves, like 'Thank you
for the cross' (Graham Kendrick) and 'Thank you, Lord,
for this fine day' (Diane Davis Andrew).

Some songs, like 'We believe in God the Father'
(Graham Kendrick), are expounding Bible truths in
prayer.

Choose the songs you prefer as you learn the Scriptures
through song and have fun. Instruments or actions can be
added as the song is learned. *Songs of Fellowship for Kids*
includes ready-made actions to thirty-nine songs.

Statement of intent

Songs can also be used as a statement of intent. For
example, the chorus in Ishmael's song 'I'm gonna say my
prayers'. As they sing, the children are reminding themselves of how to live their lives for Jesus by:

• talking to him;
• finding out how to live from the Bible;
• joining with other Christians;
• sharing the good news of Jesus . . . every day.

Further songs

Daniel was a man of prayer (*JP*)
How did Moses cross the Red Sea? (*JP*)
Peter and James and John (*JP*)
Peter and John went to pray (*JP*)
Only a boy called David (*JP*)
Our Father who is in Heaven (*JP*)
When Israel was in Egypt's land (*JP*)

Other useful songbooks are listed under Resources.

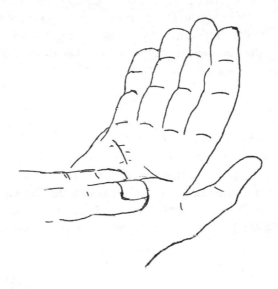

97. Sign the word

We have found that children in our local primary school enjoy using signing for the deaf as they sing. The value of deaf signing is that children are learning another language and one that communicates with those who cannot hear. It is welcoming for deaf children, and thus enables hearing and non-hearing children to worship together. Sign-singing in itself is very beautiful to watch. Signing can be used with spoken prayers too.

What you need

Someone from your church who signs
OR

A book like Richard Chubb's *Lifting Holy Hands: A Dictionary of Signs Used in Church Services* (Church House Publishing). This gives easy-to-follow diagrams for learning the specialist signs in current use in church that are not normally taught in deaf-signing classes.

Using the idea

The signs can be taught or caught! If you can sing the song or say the prayer and sign it as you do so, the children will quickly pick up the signs by copying you. If they are experiencing difficulties, then the signs can be shown on their own. Once the signs for a song are known, the children can pray the song or prayer without the words being sung or spoken.

98. Rap the word

Songs, chants, rhymes and raps all help children to recall the word of God. Some of us chanted our multiplication tables at school and this is how we recall them today. So let's rap.

What you need

A ready-made rap, or write one yourself

Using the idea

If the rap is already written, give copies to the children and rap it. For making your own, take a Bible verse or passage and use this as the basis for your rap. Speak it to yourself. The children can do this. The idea is that by speaking it out, you play with the sound of the words and with the words themselves until they fall into a rap-style pattern. The following example has been written especially for this book. It is based on Exodus 20 and took about fifteen minutes to create.

You cannot have any gods but me
    Only me, only me
You must not use God's name in vain
    Have you got it? Have you got it?
Remember, don't work on the sabbath day
    Keep it holy, keep it holy
Honour your father and your mother
    Have respect, and obey
    Or pay the price, or pay the price
Don't ever take what is not yours
    Keep your hands off, keep your hands off
Don't tell lies about your neighbours
    Tell the truth, tell the truth
When you're married to your partner
    Stay faithful, stay faithful
Be thankful to God for what you've got
    Be thankful, be thankful
Make sure the Lord's above all things
    If you've got it, say Amen!

(Hannah Dyer)

The rap can be your prayer.

99. Dance the word

Young children love to dance. Just put on some music and many will soon be moving to it. However, dance is not just for young children. Older children, teenagers and adults can dance too! Dance can be used in prayers of praise and celebration, confession, intercession, prophecy, spiritual warfare, healing, and praying the word of God. It can range from simple movements to more complex choreographed pieces. It can be solo or done as a group. Props like flags and ribbons can be used for older children (see Idea 88).

What you need

A song of your choice

Using the idea

Take a simple song based on a scripture, like 'Father we adore you' (Terrye Coelho) based on the thought behind Romans 12:1, and listen to the words. This song can be found in *Junior Praise*. Most children have experience of dance in school and so, after listening to the song and thinking about what it is saying, you can expect them to be able to experiment with moving to the song. If you are with a group of children, they could experiment on their own first. Then they can do the movements together as a group. You might start with one child's movement and then change to another child's for the next verse, and so on, or each could do their own in a way that relates to others in the group. This is dancing the word in prayer.

If the children are having difficulties, suggest they show you different ways of lifting their hands in adoration, offering themselves and showing love to God. They can then consider whether to stand or kneel – on one knee or two – look up or look down. In their group, they could think about whether they prefer to do the same movements at the same time, or each do something different. Are they all moving, or do they want to move one after the other? Are they using different levels in their movement for greater interest?

With younger children

Younger children find it hard to sit still for very long, so praying with their bodies is a good way for them to pray. Songs of praise can be times to jump and clap, to shake an instrument or wave a ribbon. Young children love to copy, so if you move to a song, you will find that they are doing the same.

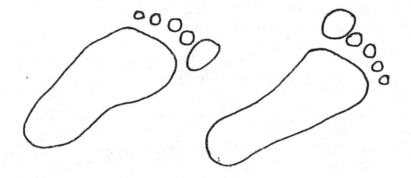

100. Take the word

In Matthew 28:19 we are commanded to go and make disciples of all nations. As the children think about God's word, one aspect is doing it. This idea uses their feet to take the word of God to others.

Footprints 1

What you need

Paper and pencil, scissors

Using the idea

The children can draw round their or a partner's feet. Get them to cut these out and lay them on the floor, leading towards the door. Add the text: 'Go, then, to all peoples everywhere and make them my disciples' (Matthew 28:19). Each word could be written on one of the feet. While they are looking at the footprints, the children can ask God to help them to tell others about Jesus:

Lord, I really want to tell others about you, but it isn't always easy. Please give me the words to say. Help me to remember too that it is not just the words I say, but the things I do, which people notice, so help me to behave in the way you want me to. Thank you, Lord. Amen.

Footprints 2

What you need

Paint, large sheet of paper, bowl of soapy water and a towel

Using the idea

One way to make a footprint poster is by getting the children to dip their feet into paint and then walk over a piece of paper. The paper can be displayed with the words of the text. This is a messy activity and, at the end, the children need to be able to step into a bowl of water to wash their feet. Make sure you use water-based paint!

Shoe rubbings

What you need

Paper, wax crayons

Using the idea

Place the paper on the bottom of the shoe and rub over with a wax crayon. Cut out and these can be used as foot-prints. Use as above.

Songs

Brothers and sisters (*JP*)
Colours of day (*JP*)
Go, go, go (*SOFK*)
Go, tell it on the mountain (*JP*)
Lord, we come in adoration (*SOFK*)

PART THREE

Resources

Books

Armstrong, Lance, *Children in Worship* (The Joint Board of Christian Education, 1988).

Chubb, Richard, *Lifting Holy Hands* (ABM Publications, 1994).

Copsey, Kathryn, *Here's One I Made Earlier* (Scripture Union, 1995).

Graystone, Peter and Turner, Eileen, *A Church for All Ages* (Scripture Union, 1993).

Hopwood, Dave and Lynn, *Telling Tales* (CPAS, 1997).

Horley, Doug, *How to be a Warrior Kid for Jesus* (Doug Horley, 1999).

Hubbard, Richard, *Taking Children Seriously* (Marshall Pickering, 1991).

Ishmael, *Angels with Dirty Faces* (Kingsway, 1989).

Johnstone, Jill, *You Can Change the World* (OM Publishing, 1992).

Kendrick, Graham and Houghton, John, *Prayerwalking* (Kingsway, 1990).

Merrell, Judith, *Pick 'n' Mix* (Scripture Union, 1997).

Neilands, Lynda, *50 Five-Minute Stories* (Kingsway, 1996).

Neilands, Lynda, *50 Stories for Special Occasions* (Kingsway, 1998).

Pinchbeck, Lesley, *Theme Games* (Scripture Union, 1993).

Price, Alan, *Children in Renewal* (Hodder & Stoughton, 1996).

Price, Sue, *100 Simple Bible Craft Ideas for Children* (Kingsway, 1998).

Relf, Sue, *100 Instant Children's Talks* (Kingsway, 1994).

Seamstress Ltd, *Playchute Games* (Seamstress Ltd, 1995).

Seamstress Ltd, *Playchute in Christian Teaching* (Seamstress Ltd, 1999).

Spraggett, Daphne, *You Too Can Change the World* (OM Publishing, 1996).

Williams, Emlyn, *The Schools Work Handbook* (Scripture Union, 1996).

Bibles

New International Version, *The Adventure Bible* (Hodder & Stoughton, 1989).

Good News Bible (Collins, 1976).

For younger children

The Beginner's Bible (Kingsway).

The Baby Bible Storybook (Kingsway).

The Toddler's Bible (Kingsway).

The Preschooler's Bible (Kingsway).

The Kid's Life Bible (Kingsway).

The Children's Discovery Bible (Kingsway).

For older children

God's Story (Kingsway, 1999).

For teenagers

New Century Version, *The Youth Bible* (Nelson Word, 1993).

Songbooks

Captain Alan, *Get on Board* (ICC, 1996).

Captain Alan, *Ready to Go* (ICC, 1998).

Captain Alan, *Salt and Light* (ICC).
Captain Alan, *Shine, Shine, Shine* (ICC).
Captain Alan, *Special Agents* (ICC).
Hardwick, John, *I'm No Cartoon* (Hardwick, 1995).
Hardwick, John, *34 Songs for All Occasions* (Hardwick, 1998).
Junior Praise (Marshall Pickering, 1986).
Songs of Fellowship for Kids (Kingsway, 1988).
Spring Harvest Kids Praise (ICC).

For younger children

Wake Up and Dance (ICC, 1993).
We Want to Shout (ICC, 1996).

Audiotapes and CDs

The music books listed above have accompanying tapes and backing tapes, and some have CDs. Individual song-writers have their own selections. For example:

Bailey, Jim, *Children of the Cross*, Cassette/CD (Kingsway).
Ishmael, *Little Songs for Little Children*, Cassette/CD (Kingsway).
Horley, Doug, *King of Heaven*, Cassette/CD (Kingsway).
Plant, Julia, *God's Wonderful World*, Cassette/CD (Kingsway).

Video

Big Idea Productions Inc., *Veggie Tales* (Word, 1994–97).
Stephenson, John, *et al*, *The Story Keepers* (Scripture Union, 1997).

Useful addresses

Children Worldwide (Resources, including puppets) 'Dalesdown', Honeybridge, Dial Post, Horsham, West Sussex RH13 8NX.

Christian Aid
PO Box 100, London SE1 7RT. Website: http://www. christian-aid.org.uk; e-mail: info@christian-aid.org

Daniel Prayer Groups for Children (King's Kids, YWAM) Stanely House, 14 Stanely Crescent, Paisley, Scotland PA2 9LF. Website: http://www.ywam.co.uk/dpghome.htm

Stopwatch
Chime (Children in Mission and Evangelism), 11a Upper Teddington Road, Kingston upon Thames, Surrey KT1 4DL. E-mail: s.kimber@chimeworldwide.clara.co.uk

Scripture Union
207–209 Queensway, Bletchley, Milton Keynes MK2 2EB. Website: http://www.scripture.org.uk

Tearfund
100 Church Road, Teddington, Middlesex TW11 8QE. Website: www.tearfund.org; e-mail: enquiry@tearfund. dircon.co.uk

Toybox Charity
PO Box 660, Amersham, Bucks HP6 6EA. Website:
www.toybox.org; e-mail: toybox@toybox.org

Captain Alan Price and **The Teknon Trust** (Children and
renewal)
PO Box 239, Derby DE22 1XH. E-mail: admin@teknon.
org

Jim Bailey, Kingdom Creative
45 Rowlands Road, Worthing, West Sussex BN11 3JN.
Website: www.kingdomc.mcmail.com; e-mail: jimbailey@
mcmail.com

Ishmael and **The Glorie Company**
Revelation Centre, P.O. Box 58, Chichester, West Sussex
PO19 2UD. Website: http://ourworld.compuserve.com/
homepages/ishmaelsmale; e-mail: ishmaelsmale@
compuserve.com

Duggie Dug Dug (Doug Horley)
P.O. Box 293, Epsom, Surrey KT19 9YE. Website: duggie
dugdug.co.uk; e-mail: duggiedugdug@clara.net

Seamstress Ltd (for playchutes)
23 Banbury Road, Byfield, Northants NN11 6XJ.

Index

314   100 CREATIVE PRAYER IDEAS FOR CHILDREN

Learning Styles

by Marlene LeFever

We know that people are different, yet so often we expect them to learn in the same way. They don't. Some respond well to our traditional teaching methods, while others struggle. Some need to talk in order to learn. Others learn best when they can move and learn at the same time. Still others remember pictures more than words. There is no 'right' way.

This book identifies four learning styles that form a Natural Learning Cycle. It shows how to involve *every* person being taught, young and old. Different students will come to the fore at different times in the lesson, depending on the basic question they are asking:

- Why do I need to know this? (*'Imaginative'*)
- What are the facts? (*'Analytic'*)
- How will it work? (*'Common sense'*)
- How can I develop what I have learned? (*'Dynamic'*)

 **Kingsway Publications**

100 Simple Bible Craft Ideas for Children

by Sue Price

Many of us learn more effectively when we have something to see and something to make; when we can interact rather than simply sit and listen.

Crafts can therefore be used as a vital part of any session with children, and not just an add-on. This collection of illustrated ideas has been specifically designed to help children learn stories and truths from the Bible in such a way that they can make them part of their lives. They are ideal for teachers who would not regard themselves as experts, yet can easily be adapted by the more experienced!

The ideas have been grouped according to categories:

- Bible stories
- Lesson reminders
- Aids to worship
- Crafts to give
- Seasonal items

 **Kingsway Publications**

100 Instant Ideas for All-Age Worship

by Sue Relf

Having people of all ages together for any length of structured time can be a challenge. This book provides a wealth of 'pick and mix' ideas for those involved in leading all-age worship, including:

- Mini-talks
- Dramas
- Bible readings
- Raps
- Praise and worship
- Prayers
- Testimonies
- Quizzes

Sue Relf's experience in leading family services, Bible clubs and camps has made her aware of the need for lots of ideas that are quick to prepare and easy to illustrate. She is also the author of the bestselling *100 Instant Children's Talks*.

 Kingsway Publications

50 Stories for Special Occasions

by Lynda Neilands

Good stories teach values, touch the emotions, foster empathy, lodge in the memory and can be a powerful vehicle for spiritual truth.

This is a book of stories for telling to children. Divided into sections, one for each month of the year, here you will find stories appropriate for:

- Christmas
- Easter, Harvest
- Valentine's Day
- Mothering Sunday
- Bible Sunday
- Father's Day

...and many more!

Each story is accompanied by an application, teaching point, Bible reading and a list of relevant songs.

 Kingsway Publications